EXCEL
FOR
WINDOWS® 95
FOR
DUMMIES®

by John Walkenbach

IDG
BOOKS
WORLDWIDE

IDG Books Worldwide, Inc.
An International Data Group Company

Foster City, CA ◆ Chicago, IL ◆ Indianapolis, IN
Braintree, MA ◆ Southlake, TX

Excel For Windows® 95 For Dummies® Quick Reference

Published by
IDG Books Worldwide, Inc.
An International Data Group Company
919 E. Hillsdale Blvd., Suite 400
Foster City, CA 94404

Library of Congress Catalog Card No.: 95-81099

ISBN: 1-56884-976-1

Printed in the United States of America

10 9 8 7 6 5 4 3

1A/SR/QV/ZW/IN

Distributed in the United States by IDG Books Worldwide, Inc.

Distributed by Macmillan Canada for Canada; by Computer and Technical Books for the Caribbean Basin; by Contemporanea de Ediciones for Venezuela; by Distribuidora Cuspide for Argentina; by CITEC for Brazil; by Ediciones ZETA S.C.R. Ltda. for Peru; by Editorial Limusa SA for Mexico; by Transworld Publishers Limited in the United Kingdom and Europe; by Al-Maiman Publishers & Distributors for Saudi Arabia; by Simron Pty. Ltd. for South Africa; by IDG Communications (HK) Ltd. for Hong Kong; by Toppan Company Ltd. for Japan; by Addison Wesley Publishing Company for Korea; by Longman Singapore Publishers Ltd. for Singapore, Malaysia, Thailand, and Indonesia; by Unalis Corporation for Taiwan; by WS Computer Publishing Company, Inc. for the Philippines; by WoodsLane Pty. Ltd. for Australia; by WoodsLane Enterprises Ltd. for New Zealand.

For general information on IDG Books Worldwide's books in the U.S., please call our Consumer Customer Service department at 800-762-2974. For reseller information, including discounts and premium sales, please call our Reseller Customer Service department at 800-434-3422.

For information on where to purchase IDG Books Worldwide's books outside the U.S., contact IDG Books Worldwide at 415-655-3021 or fax 415-655-3295.

For information on translations, contact Marc Jeffrey Mikulich, Director, Foreign & Subsidiary Rights, at IDG Books Worldwide, 415-655-3018 or fax 415-655-3295.

For sales inquiries and special prices for bulk quantities, write to the address above or call IDG Books Worldwide at 415-655-3200.

For information on using IDG Books Worldwide's books in the classroom, or ordering examination copies, contact the Education Office at 800-434-2086 or fax 817-251-8174.

For authorization to photocopy items for corporate, personal, or educational use, please contact Copyright Clearance Center, 222 Rosewood Drive, Danvers, MA 01923, or fax 508-750-4470.

About the Author

John Walkenbach

John Walkenbach is one of the country's leading authorities on spreadsheet software. He holds a Ph.D. from the University of Montana and has worked as an instructor, programmer, and market research manager at a large bank. He finally found a job he's good at: principal of JWalk and Associates Inc., a one-person San Diego-based consulting firm that specializes in spreadsheet application development. John is also a shareware developer, and his most popular product is the Power Utility Pak add-in for Excel — which is used by thousands of people throughout the world. John started writing about spreadsheets in 1984 and has since written more than 250 articles and reviews for publications such as *PC World, InfoWorld, Windows,* and *PC/Computing.* In addition, he's the author of a dozen or so other spreadsheet books, including *Excel for Windows 95 Bible* and *Excel 5 for Windows Power Programming Techniques* (both from IDG Books Worldwide, Inc.). In his spare time, John enjoys composing and playing music in a variety of styles, including blues, bluegrass, and new age. You can reach John on the Internet at 70363.3014@compuserve.com.

ABOUT IDG BOOKS WORLDWIDE

Welcome to the world of IDG Books Worldwide.

IDG Books Worldwide, Inc., is a subsidiary of International Data Group, the world's largest publisher of computer-related information and the leading global provider of information services on information technology. IDG was founded more than 25 years ago and now employs more than 7,700 people worldwide. IDG publishes more than 250 computer publications in 67 countries (see listing below). More than 70 million people read one or more IDG publications each month.

Launched in 1990, IDG Books Worldwide is today the #1 publisher of best-selling computer books in the United States. We are proud to have received 8 awards from the Computer Press Association in recognition of editorial excellence and three from Computer Currents' First Annual Readers' Choice Awards, and our best-selling ...For Dummies® series has more than 19 million copies in print with translations in 28 languages. IDG Books Worldwide, through a joint venture with IDG's Hi-Tech Beijing, became the first U.S. publisher to publish a computer book in the People's Republic of China. In record time, IDG Books Worldwide has become the first choice for millions of readers around the world who want to learn how to better manage their businesses.

Our mission is simple: Every one of our books is designed to bring extra value and skill-building instructions to the reader. Our books are written by experts who understand and care about our readers. The knowledge base of our editorial staff comes from years of experience in publishing, education, and journalism — experience which we use to produce books for the '90s. In short, we care about books, so we attract the best people. We devote special attention to details such as audience, interior design, use of icons, and illustrations. And because we use an efficient process of authoring, editing, and desktop publishing our books electronically, we can spend more time ensuring superior content and spend less time on the technicalities of making books.

You can count on our commitment to deliver high-quality books at competitive prices on topics you want to read about. At IDG Books Worldwide, we continue in the IDG tradition of delivering quality for more than 25 years. You'll find no better book on a subject than one from IDG Books Worldwide.

John J Kilcullen

John Kilcullen
President and CEO
IDG Books Worldwide, Inc.

WINNER
Eighth Annual
Computer Press
Awards ≩ 1992

WINNER
Ninth Annual
Computer Press
Awards ≩ 1993

IDG Books Worldwide, Inc., is a subsidiary of International Data Group, the world's largest publisher of computer-related information and the leading global provider of information services on information technology. International Data Group publishes over 250 computer publications in 67 countries. Seventy million people read one or more International Data Group publications each month. International Data Group's publications include: ARGENTINA: Computerworld Argentina, GamePro, Infoworld, PC World Argentina; AUSTRALIA: Australian Macworld, Client/Server Journal, Computer Living, Computerworld, Digital News, Network World, PC World, Publishing Essentials, Reseller; AUSTRIA: Computerwelt, PC TEST; BELARUS: PC World Belarus; BELGIUM: Data News; BRAZIL: Annuário de Informática, Computerworld Brazil, Connections, Super Game Power, Macworld, PC World Brazil, Publish Brazil, SUPERGAME; BULGARIA: Computerworld Bulgaria, Networkworld/Bulgaria, PC & MacWorld Bulgaria; CANADA: CIO Canada, ComputerWorld Canada, InfoCanada, Network World Canada, Reseller World; CHILE: Computerworld Chile, GamePro, PC World Chile; COLUMBIA: Computerworld Colombia, GamePro, PC World Colombia; COSTA RICA: PC World Costa Rica/Nicaragua; THE CZECH AND SLOVAK REPUBLICS: Computerworld Czechoslovakia, Elektronika Czechoslovakia, PC World Czechoslovakia; DENMARK: Communications World, Computerworld Danmark, Macworld Danmark, PC World Danmark, PC World Danmark Supplements, TECH World; DOMINICAN REPUBLIC: PC World Republica Dominicana; ECUADOR: PC World Ecuador, GamePro; EGYPT: Computerworld Middle East, PC World Middle East; EL SALVADOR: PC World Centro America; FINLAND: MikroPC, Tietoverkko, Tietoviikko; FRANCE: Distributique, Golden, Info PC, Le Guide du Monde Informatique, Le Monde Informatique, Reseaux & Telecoms; GERMANY: Computer Business, Computerworld, Computerwoche Extra, Computerwoche Focus, Electronic Entertainment, GamePro, I/M Information Management, Macwelt, PC Welt; GREECE: GamePro, Macworld & Publish; GUATEMALA: PC World Centro America; HONDURAS: PC World Centro America; HONG KONG: Computerworld Hong Kong, PCWorld Hong Kong, Publish in Asia; HUNGARY: ABCD CD-ROM, Computerworld Szamitastechnika, PC & Mac World Hungary, PC-X Magazine; INDIA: Computerworld India, PC World India, Publish in Asia; INDONESIA: InfoKomputer PC World, Komputek Computerworld, Publish in Asia; IRELAND: ComputerScope, PC Live!; ISRAEL: PC World 32 BIT, People & Computers; ITALY: Computerworld Italia, Computerworld Italia Special Editions, Lotus Italia, Macworld Italia, Networking Italia, PC Shopping, PC World Italia, PC World/Walt Disney; JAPAN: Macworld Japan, Nikkei Personal Computing, SunWorld Japan, Windows World Japan; KENYA: East African Computer News; KOREA: Hi-Tech Information/Computerworld, Macworld Korea, PC World Korea; MACEDONIA: PC World Macedonia; MALAYSIA: Computerworld Malaysia, PC World Malaysia, Publish in Asia; MEXICO: Computerworld Mexico, GamePro, Macworld, PC World Mexico; MYANMAR: PC World Myanmar; NETHERLANDS: Computable, Computer! Totaal, LAN Magazine, Macworld, Net Magazine; NEW ZEALAND: Computer Buyer, Computerworld New Zealand, MTB, Network World, PC World New Zealand; NICARAGUA: PC World Costa Rica/Nicaragua; NIGERIA: PC World Africa; NORWAY: Computerworld Norge, Computerworld Privat, CW Rapport Klient/Tjener, CW Rapport Nettverk & Telecom, CW Rapport Offentlig Sektor, IDG's KUSSGUIDE, Macworld Norge, Multimedia World, PC World Ekspress, PC World Nettverk, PC World Norge, PC World's Produktguide, Windows Spesial; PAKISTAN: Computerworld Pakistan, PC World Pakistan; PANAMA: GamePro, PC World Panama; PARAGUAY: PC World Paraguay; P R OF CHINA: China Computerworld, China Infoworld, Computer & Communication, Electronic Product World, Electronics Today, Game Camp, PC World China, Popular Computer Week, Software World, Telecom Product World; PERU: Computerworld Peru, GamePro, PC World Profesional Peru, PC World Peru; POLAND: Computerworld Poland, Computerworld Special Report, Macworld, Networld, PC World Komputer; PHILIPPINES: Computerworld Philippines, PC Digest, Publish in Asia; PORTUGAL: Cerebro/PC World, Correio Informático/Computerworld, Mac•In/PC•In Portugal; PUERTO RICO: PC World Puerto Rico; ROMANIA: Computerworld Romania, PC World Romania, Telecom Romania; RUSSIA: Computerworld Rossiya, Network World Russia, PC World Russia; SINGAPORE: Computerworld Singapore, PC World Singapore, Publish in Asia; SLOVENIA: MONITOR; SOUTH AFRICA: Computing S.A., Network World S.A., Software World; SPAIN: Computerworld España, COMUNICACIONES WORLD, Dealer World, Macworld España, PC World España; SWEDEN: CAP&Design, Computer Sweden, Corporate Computing, MacWorld, Maxi Data, MikroDatorn, Nätverk & Kommunikation, PC/Aktiv, PC World, Windows World; SWITZERLAND: Computerworld Schweiz, Macworld Schweiz, PCtip; TAIWAN: Computerworld Taiwan, Macworld Taiwan, PC World Taiwan, Publish Taiwan, Windows World; THAILAND: Thai Computerworld, Publish in Asia; TURKEY: Computerworld Monitor, MACWORLD Türkiye, PC WORLD Türkiye; UKRAINE: Computerworld Kiev, Computers & Software Magazine, PC World Ukraine; UNITED KINGDOM: Acorn User, Amiga Action, Amiga Computing, Amiga, Appletalk, CD Powerplay, CD-ROM Now, Computing, Connexion, GamePro, Lotus Magazine, Macaction, Macworld, Open Computing, Parents and Computers, PC Home, PC Works, The WEB; UNITED STATES: Cable in the Classroom, CD Review, CIO Magazine, Computerworld, Computerworld Client/Server Journal, Digital Video Magazine, DOS World, Electronic, InfoWorld, I-Way, Macworld, Maximize, MULTIMEDIA WORLD, Network World, PC World, PUBLISH, SWATPro Magazine, Video Event, WebMaster; URUGUAY: PC World Uruguay; VENEZUELA: Computerworld Venezuela, GamePro, PC World Venezuela; and VIETNAM: PC World Vietnam   10/17/95

Dedication

Yet another book dedicated to VaRene.

Publisher's Acknowledgments

We're proud of this book; send us your comments about it by using the
Reader Response Card at the back of the book or by e-mailing us at
feedback/dummies@idgbooks.com. Some of the people who helped
bring this book to market include:

Acquisitions, Development,
& Editorial

Project Editor: Kathleen M. Cox

Product Development Manager:
Mary Bednarek

Copy Editor: Suzanne Packer

Technical Reviewer: Jim McCarter

Editorial Managers: Kristin A. Cocks,
Mary C. Corder

Editorial Assistants:
Constance Carlisle,
Chris H. Collins, Jerelind Davis

Special Help

Editorial Executive Assistant:
Richard Graves

Production

Project Coordinator: Valery Bourke

Layout and Graphics:
E. Shawn Aylsworth,
Cameron Booker,
Elizabeth Cárdenas-Nelson,
Michael Sullivan, Angela F. Hunckler,
Gina Scott, Carla Radzikinas

Proofreaders: Jenny Kaufeld,
Christine Meloy Beck,
Gwenette Gaddis, Dwight Ramsey,
Carl Saff, Robert Springer

Indexer: Sharon Hilgenberg

General & Administrative

IDG Books Worldwide, Inc.: John Kilcullen, President & CEO;
Steven Berkowitz, COO & Publisher

Dummies, Inc.: Milissa Koloski, Executive Vice President & Publisher

Dummies Technology Press & Dummies Editorial: Diane Graves Steele, Associate
Publisher; Judith A. Taylor, Brand Manager; Myra Immell, Editorial Director

Dummies Trade Press: Kathleen A. Welton, Vice President & Publisher;
Stacy S. Collins, Brand Manager

IDG Books Production for Dummies Press: Beth Jenkins, Production Director;
Cindy L. Phipps, Supervisor of Project Coordination; Kathie S. Schnorr,
Supervisor of Page Layout; Shelley Lea, Supervisor of Graphics and Design

Dummies Packaging & Book Design: Erin McDermitt, Packaging Coordinator;
Kavish+Kavish, Cover Design

◆

The publisher would like to give special thanks to Patrick J. McGovern,
without whom this book would not have been possible.

◆

Acknowledgments

Thanks to all of the folks at IDG Books who helped transform hundreds of thousands of bytes on my hard disk into a real book. I'm particularly grateful to Kathy Cox, my project editor, Suzanne Packer, the copy editor, and all the others behind the scenes who pulled it all together. Thanks also to Jim McCarter for a thorough technical review.

The following all made this task a bit easier: Howard Stern (for giving me a good reason to get an early start in the morning), Music Choice (a cable music service that provided nonstop blues and jazz during the post-Howard hours), C.F. Martin & Co. (for making a great HD-28 to entertain me during work breaks), and Microsoft Corporation (for giving me something good to write about).

And once again, thanks to my best friend VaRene for keeping me company and providing lots of good times and support.

(The Publisher would like to give special thanks to Patrick J. McGovern, without whom this book would not have been possible.)

Table of Contents

Part III: Formatting, Outlining, and Printing Your Work 39

Part IV: Entering and Editing Worksheet Data .. 71

Part V: Using Formulas and Functions 97

How to Use This Book

Greetings. You're holding in your hands one of a different breed of computer reference books — a book written for normal people (not computer geeks). The *Excel For Windows 95 For Dummies Quick Reference* is for those of you who have no aspirations of becoming a spreadsheet wizard. Rather, you want to be able to do your job efficiently so that you can move on to more important things — like having a life.

This book: Who needs it?

I wrote this book for the hundreds of thousands of beginning to intermediate Excel users who have better things to do with their time than wade through technical dribble just to figure out how to do something so they can go home.

When I was asked to write this book, I visited several local book stores to get an idea of what I would be competing with for shelf space. I found dozens of Excel books and Excel command reference guides. With a few exceptions, these books are boring, too technical, and not much fun to read. One such exception to this state of affairs is Greg Harvey's *Excel For Windows 95 For Dummies*. If you have absolutely no experience with Excel, Greg's book is a good place to start. My book is designed to go hand-in-hand with it — or stand alone. My suggestion? Buy them both.

Excel can be used at many different levels, and it's a safe bet that the majority of Excel users don't really have a clue as to what the program can really do when all the stops are pulled out. My goal is to open the door to some of the cool things that Excel can do — and do so in a way that doesn't put you to sleep.

On the one hand, Excel is very easy to use. I can spend 20 minutes with a new user and have them doing semi-useful things by themselves afterward. But practically all Excel users eventually reach a head-scratching point when they want to do something, but can't figure out how. This book should come to the rescue.

The truth of the matter is that virtually no one actually needs or uses *all* of the Excel commands. Most users get by just fine after they learn the basics. But if you stick to the basics, you run the risk of causing more work for yourself. For example, Excel has commands that automate things that may take you an hour to do manually. Saving ten minutes here or half an hour there adds up. You'll have more time for fun things and can maybe even get out of the office at a reasonable hour — not to mention the fact that people will be amazed at how efficient you've become.

Ways to use this book

This book is organized into nine parts. Topics in each part are alphabetized by task, and each task is designed as a self-contained unit. In other words, the book is intended to minimize the amount of reading you have to do.

You can use this book in several ways:

+ If you need to find out how to do something in Excel, look up the general topic in the Table of Contents and see if it sounds like what you want to accomplish. If so, turn to that part and find the appropriate section.

+ If you don't even have a clue as to the proper command to look up, head for the index and look at words that describe what you want to do. This usually steers you to the section that you're looking for.

✦ If you find yourself with a spare hour or two while circling over LAX waiting to land, browse through this book and read things that are interesting to you. You just may discover something that you didn't know Excel could do — and it's just what you need for a project you're working on.

✦ Keep this book laying around on your desk. That way, people will come by and make some sort of comment about the title of the book. This will inevitably lead to disparaging remarks about your intelligence level. The ensuing conversation is a good way to kill some time when you should be working.

How not to use this book

Whatever you do, don't read this book from cover to cover. Frankly, the plot stinks, the character development leaves much to be desired, and you'll be disappointed by the ending. Although it's moderately entertaining, the book is not exactly what you would call a page-turner.

What the Little Pictures Mean

All the good computer books have little icons sprinkled liberally throughout their pages. These icons work great for visually oriented people and tell you in an instant a few key things about each command. Here's what the icons in this book mean:

This icon flags a command that is available only if you've loaded a particular add-in file.

This icon signals the fastest and most efficient way to perform a task. Often, the fastest way is to use a toolbox button. In that case, you'll just see the button.

This icon flags problem areas that can mess up your work if you're not on your toes.

This icon flags a way of using the command that may not be immediately obvious to the average bear.

This icon indicates a feature that is available only in Excel for Windows 95.

Important Note: This book covers Excel for Windows 95. Most of the book is also relevant to Excel 5, but the latest version has a few new features, which I point out in the text.

Part 1

Getting to Know Excel 95

Excel is one of several spreadsheet programs that software vendors try to get you to buy. Other spreadsheets that you may have heard of include Lotus 1-2-3 for Windows and Novell's Quattro Pro for Windows. Many others have come and gone over the years, but these are by far the most popular ones.

In this part . . .

✓ **Cells and ranges**

✓ **Checking out the Excel screen**

✓ **Using Excel commands**

✓ **Dialog boxes and toolbars**

✓ **Using Excel add-ins**

Excel: Behind the Scenes

A spreadsheet program is essentially a highly interactive environment that lets you work with numbers and text in a large grid of cells. Excel also creates graphs and maps from numbers stored in a worksheet and works with database information stored in a record and field format.

Excel's files are known as workbooks. A single workbook can store as many sheets as will fit into memory, and these sheets are stacked like the pages in a notebook. Sheets can be any of the following:

✦ Worksheets

✦ Chart sheets

✦ Excel 4.0 macro sheets (for compatibility with older versions)

✦ Visual Basic (VBA) module sheets

✦ Dialog sheets

Most of the time, you'll be working with worksheets — each of which has exactly 16,384 rows and 256 columns. Rows are numbered from 1 to 16,384, and columns are labeled with letters. Column 1 is A, column 26 is Z, column 27 is AA, column 52 is AZ, column 53 is BZ, and so on up to column 256 (which is IV).

The intersection of a row and column is called a *cell*. My calculator tells me that this works out to 4,194,304 cells — which should be enough for most people. Cells have addresses, which are based on the row and column in which they are located. The upper-left cell in a worksheet is called A1, and the cell way down at the bottom is called IV256. Cell K9 (also known as the dog cell) is the intersection of the eleventh column and the ninth row.

A cell in Excel can hold a number, some text, a formula, or nothing at all. You already know what numbers and text are, but you may be a bit fuzzy on the concept of a formula. A *formula* is a special way to tell Excel to perform a calculation using information stored in other cells. For example, you can insert a formula that tells Excel to add up the values in the first 10 cells in column A and to display the result in the cell that has the formula.

Formulas can use normal arithmetic operators such as + (plus), - (minus), * (multiply), and / (divide). They can also use special built-in functions that let you do powerful things without much effort on your part. For example, Excel has functions that add up a range of values, calculate square roots, compute loan payments, and even tell you the time of day. Using Excel's functions is covered in Part V.

When you create a chart from numbers stored in a worksheet, you can put the chart directly on the worksheet or in a special chart sheet in the workbook. When you're working with a chart, some of Excel's menus change so that they are appropriate for chart-type operations.

A new feature in Excel 95 lets you create maps using data stored in a worksheet. Maps reside on a worksheet (there's no such thing as a map sheet). Maps are handy for showing information based on geography, such as sales by state.

The active cell and ranges

In Excel, one of the cells in a worksheet is always the *active cell*. The active cell is selected and is displayed with a thicker border. Its contents appear in the formula bar, located at the top of the Excel window under the menu bar. You can also select a group of cells by clicking and dragging the mouse over them. The selected cells are highlighted on the screen. When you issue a command that does something to a cell or a range of.cells, that something will be done to the active cell or to the selected range of cells.

The selected *range* is usually a group of contiguous cells, but it doesn't have to be. If you hold down the Ctrl key while you click and drag the mouse, you can select more than one group of cells. Then, commands you issue will work on all of the selected cells.

Navigational techniques

With more than 4 million cells in a worksheet, you need ways to move to specific cells. Fortunately, Excel provides you with many techniques to move around through a worksheet. As always, you can use either your mouse or the keyboard on your navigational journeys. The navigational keys are covered in Part II.

The Excel Screen

The following figure shows a typical Excel screen, with some of the important parts pointed out. This terminology will rear its ugly head throughout this book, so pay attention.

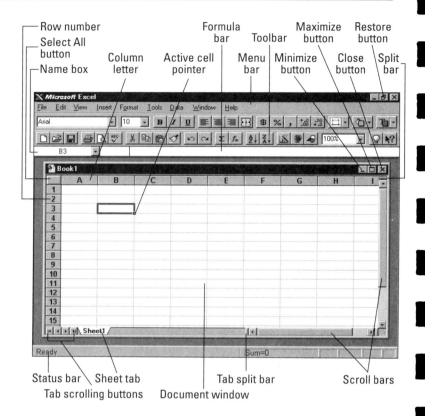

Row number — Select All button — Name box | Column letter | Active cell pointer | Formula bar | Toolbar | Menu bar | Maximize button | Minimize button | Restore button | Close button | Split bar

Status bar | Sheet tab | Tab scrolling buttons | Tab split bar | Document window | Scroll bars

Excel Commands

Excel has many commands that you use to do the things that spreadsheet users do. Here's a typical Excel command: File⇨Open. This command opens a workbook file so that you can work in it.

You can invoke this command in several different ways:

✦ Click the File menu with the mouse and then click the Open command.

✦ Press Alt+F (for File) and then O (for Open).

✦ Press Alt or F10 to activate the menu bar; then use the arrow keys to move to the File menu. Press Enter and use the arrow keys to move to the Open command. Press Enter again to issue the command.

✦ Click the button on the Standard toolbar that looks like a file folder opening up.

✦ Press Ctrl+F12 (or Alt+Ctrl+F2 if your keyboard lacks an F12 function key).

All of these techniques have the same result: The Open dialog box pops up. This dialog box lets you tell Excel which file you want to open. Once the dialog box is displayed, you can use your mouse or keyboard to carry on the dialog and tell Excel what you're trying to do.

While having all of these command options available may seem a bit confusing, you certainly don't have to know them all. Most people simply know one method and stick to it. Also, not all commands have so many options. Because opening files is done so frequently, Excel designers went overboard and came up with several ways to do it.

Most commands lead to a dialog box, but some commands do their thing immediately with no additional work required on your part. You can tell the commands that lead to a dialog box because they are followed by ellipses (...) in the drop-down menu.

You can issue commands in Excel yet another way. Right-clicking (clicking on the right mouse button) an object, an individual cell, or a selected range of cells displays a shortcut menu that lists common commands that are appropriate to the selection. The following figure shows the shortcut menu that appears when you right-click after selecting a range of cells.

Working with Dialog Boxes

Excel, like virtually every other Windows application, is big on dialog boxes. A *dialog box* is a small window that pops up in response to most of the commands that you issue. This window is displayed right on top of what you're doing — a sure sign that you must make some type of response to the dialog box before you can do anything else.

The following figure shows a typical Excel dialog box. This particular dialog box is displayed when you select the File⇨Page Setup command. I chose this for an example because it contains many (but not all) of the types of dialog box controls that you're likely to encounter.

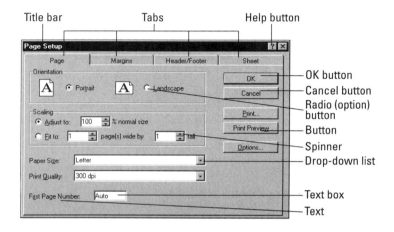

Dialog box parts

Here's a fairly exhaustive list of the various types of controls and other parts you'll meet up with as you discover the world of dialog boxes.

Button: Clicking a dialog box button does something else (the "something" depends on the button).

Cancel button: Click this if you change your mind. None of the changes you made to the dialog box will take effect.

Check box (not shown): A square that you can click to turn the option on or off.

Drop-down list: A list of things you can choose from. These lists have a small downward-point arrow. Click the arrow to drop the list down.

Help button: Click here and then click a dialog box control to learn what the control does.

List box (not shown): This shows several items to choose from and usually has a vertical scroll bar that you can click on to show more items in the list.

OK button: Click this when you have made your dialog box selections and want to get on with it.

Radio (option) buttons: Round buttons, usually enclosed in a group box. Only one option button can be "on" at a time. When you click a radio button, the others in the group are turned off.

Spinner: A control with two arrows (one pointing up, the other pointing down) used in conjunction with a text box. Clicking the arrow increases or decreases the number in the text box.

Tab: Clicking a tab changes the dialog box to display a whole new set of controls. Not all dialog boxes have these tabs.

Text box: A box in which you enter something — a number or text.

Text: Words that explain what to do. You can click on dialog box text, but nothing happens.

Title bar: The colored bar at the top of the dialog box. Click and drag this to move the dialog box to a different part of the screen if it's covering up something you want to see.

Navigating through dialog boxes

You can work with a dialog box using your mouse or the keyboard. If you use a mouse, simply position the mouse pointer on the option you want to work with and click. The exact procedure varies with the type of control, but it's quite straightforward — and all Windows programs work the same way.

You'll notice that the various parts of a dialog box have text with a single underlined letter. You can use the Alt key along with this letter to jump to that particular component. For example, the Page Setup dialog box has a text box that's preceded by text that reads, First Page Number. Because the r is underlined, pressing Alt+R puts the cursor in the text box so that you can type your option. Besides using Alt key combinations, you can use Tab and Shift+Tab to cycle through all of the controls in a dialog box.

Mousing Around with Toolbars

Among the greatest time-saving features in Excel are its toolbars. Excel comes with 13 toolbars, each of which has a bunch of buttons that provide shortcuts for commonly used commands and procedures. For example, there's a button to left-align the contents of a cell or range. Clicking a button is *much* faster than issuing the Format⇨Cells command, choosing the Alignment tab, and then selecting the Left option in the dialog box. To make a long story short, it's well worth your effort to learn about Excel's toolbars.

Actually Doing Things with Excel

The process of using Excel involves entering data and formulas into cells, manipulating the data in various ways using the menu commands and dialog boxes, and then printing the results on paper for the rest of the world to enjoy. And if you're smart, you'll take advantage of the toolbar buttons, shortcut keys, and shortcut menus to make the process even easier. Not coincidentally, all of these things are covered in the rest of this book.

Using Add-Ins

To install missing add-ins, rerun Excel's Setup program (or the Microsoft Office Setup program). To open an add-in, select Tools⊃Add-Ins and click OK.

Access Links Add-In: Lets you use Microsoft Access forms and reports with Excel worksheets.

Analysis ToolPak and ToolPak — VBA: Statistical and engineering tools plus VBA functions.

AutoSave: Automatically saves your workbook at a specified time interval.

MS Query Add-In: Works with Microsoft Query to bring external data into a worksheet.

ODBC Add-In: Lets you use ODBC (Open Database Connectivity) functions to connect to external data sources directly.

Report Manager: Prints reports that consist of a set sequence of views and scenarios.

Solver Add-In: Helps you use a variety of numeric methods for equation solving and optimization.

Template Wizard with Data Tracking: Creates custom templates.

Update Add-in Links: Updates links to MS Excel 4.0 add-ins if you open a workbook saved in Excel 4.0 that uses an older add-in.

View Manager: Creates, stores, and displays different worksheet views.

Part II

Using Workbook Files and Worksheets

Working with files is critical to using any software. Excel files are known as *workbooks*. This part covers the procedures that you need to know in order to manage workbook files and use workbooks and worksheets efficiently.

In this part . . .

 ✓ Creating, opening, and saving Excel workbooks

 ✓ Importing and exporting files

 ✓ Using workspace and template files

 ✓ Working with sheets in a workbook

 ✓ Workbook navigation techniques

Closing a Workbook

When you're finished using a workbook, use any of these methods to close it and free up the memory it uses.

✦ Use the File⇨Close command.

 ✦ Click the Close button in the workbook's title bar.

 ✦ Double-click the Control button in the workbook's title bar.

✦ Press Ctrl+F4.

✦ Press Ctrl+W.

If you've made any changes to your workbook since it was last saved, Excel asks if you want to save the changes before closing it.

 To close all open workbooks, press the Shift key and choose the File⇨Close All command (this command only appears when you hold down the Shift key while you click the File menu). Excel closes each workbook, prompting you for each unsaved workbook.

Creating an Empty Workbook File

When you start Excel, it automatically creates a new (empty) workbook called Book1. If you're starting a new project from scratch you can use this blank workbook.

You can create another workbook in one of three ways:

✦ Use the File⇨New command.

 ✦ Click the New button on the Standard toolbar.

✦ Press Ctrl+N.

You'll see the New dialog box, which lets you choose a template for the new workbook.

Most of the time, you'll just select the Workbook icon, which creates a blank default workbook. This bypasses the New dialog box and creates a new default workbook immediately.

Creating Your Own Workbook Template

A *workbook template* is a normal workbook that is used as the basis for other workbooks. A workbook template can use any of Excel's features such as charts, formulas, and macros. Normally, you set up a template so that you can enter some values and get immediate results.

To save a workbook as a template:

1. Choose the File⇨Save As command.

2. Select Template (*.xlt) from the drop-down list box labeled Save as type.

3. Save the template in your Templates folder (or a folder within the Templates folder).

Creating a Workbook from a Template

A *template* is basically a worksheet that's all set up with formulas and ready for you to enter data. The Spreadsheet Solutions templates distributed with Excel are nicely formatted and relatively easy to customize. When you open a new workbook based on the template, you save the workbook to a new file so that you don't overwrite the template.

To create a workbook from a template:

1. Select the File⇨New command or press Ctrl+N.

Excel responds by displaying the New dialog box.

2. Select the template that you want.

To use one of the Spreadsheet Solutions templates, click the Spreadsheet Solutions tab in the New dialog box. This displays a list of all of the templates available in that folder.

3. Click OK.

Deleting a Workbook File

When you no longer need a workbook file, you may want to delete it from your disk to free up space and reduce the number of files displayed in the Open dialog box.

You can delete files using Windows 95, or you can delete files directly from Excel.

1. Use either the File⇨Open command or the File⇨Save As command to bring up a dialog box with a list of filenames.

2. Right-click a filename and choose Delete from the shortcut menu.

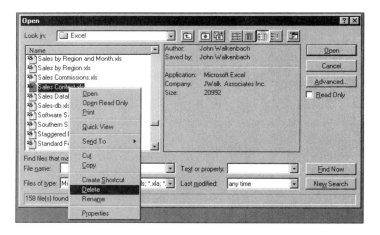

If your system is set up to use the Recycle Bin, you may be able to recover a file that was deleted accidentally.

Exporting a Text File

If you want to save information in a worksheet so that it can be used by other programs, you can export your worksheet as a text file. Most applications can read text files. To export a worksheet as a text file:

1. Choose the File⇨Save As command.

2. Select one of the following file types from the Save file as type drop-down list box: Formatted text, Text, or CSV.

3. Click Save to create the text file.

When you save a workbook as a text file, be aware that text files simply contain data; there are no formatting, formulas, or charts.

Finding a Workbook File

It's not uncommon to "lose" a file. Fortunately, Excel makes it fairly easy to locate files.

The searching all takes place from the Open dialog box (Ctrl+O brings up this dialog box). You can search for files based on the name of the file, type of file, text contained in the file, properties associated with the file, or when the file was last modified.

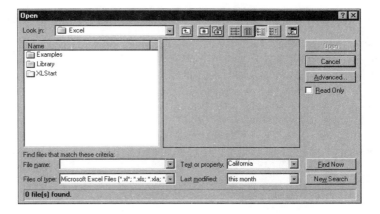

1. Specify the search scope in the Look in field. The search scope can be very broad (My Computer) or quite narrow (a single folder).

2. Determine how you want to search and fill in the appropriate field(s) at the bottom of the dialog box.

If you aren't sure of the exact filename, use wildcard characters to specify an approximate match. Use a question mark (?) as a placeholder for a single character and an asterisk (*) as a placeholder for any number of characters.

3. To start the search, click the Find Now button.

Excel eventually displays a list of files that match your criteria.

Importing a Text File

To import a text file into Excel:

1. Choose the File⇨Open command.

2. Select Text Files in the drop-down list box labeled Files of type.

The Open dialog box then displays text files that have an extension of PRN, TXT, or CSV.

3. If the text file that you're importing doesn't have one of the extensions listed in Step 2, select the All Files option.

4. Select the file and click Open.

Excel examines the file:

✦ If the file is a tab-delimited or a comma-separated value (CSV) file, Excel often imports it with no further intervention on your part.

✦ If the file can be imported in several different ways or if there are no delimiters, Excel displays its Text Import Wizard (a series of interactive dialog boxes in which you specify the information needed to break the lines of the text file into columns).

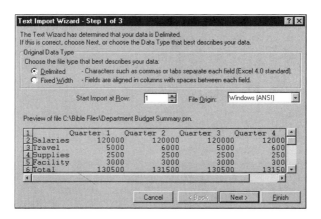

✦ To bypass the Text Import Wizard, press Shift when you click on Open in the Open dialog box. Excel then makes its best guess as to how to import the file.

If the data in the text file is not laid out in a regular manner:

1. Import the file into a single column.

2. Use the Data⇨Text to Columns command to analyze the data and parse it into columns.

Mailing a Workbook File

To send a copy of your workbook to one or more colleagues who are reachable via electronic mail:

1. Use the File⇨Send command or use the Send Mail button on the WorkGroup toolbar.

If you're using Microsoft Exchange, you need to select a profile.

2. Enter the name of the recipient (or recipients) and a message.

3. Click the Send button.

Remember: This procedure creates an e-mail message with a *copy* of your workbook attached. If the recipient makes changes to the workbook, they do not appear in your copy of the workbook.

See also "Routing a Workbook," in this part.

Opening a Foreign File

To open a non-Excel file:

1. Choose File⇨Open to bring up the Open dialog box.

2. Select the file type from the Files of type drop-down list box.

3. Specify the folder that contains the file.

4. Select the file and click Open or double-click the filename.

File Type	Description
WKS	1-2-3 Release 1 spreadsheet format*
WKS	MS Works 2.0 format*
WK1	1-2-3 Release 2 spreadsheet format**
WK3	1-2-3 Release 3 spreadsheet format**
WK4	1-2-3 for Windows spreadsheet format
WQ1	Quattro Pro for DOS spreadsheet format
DBF	dBase database format
SLK	SYLK spreadsheet format
WB1	Quattro Pro for Windows spreadsheet format
CSV	Comma-separated value text file format
TXT	Text file format
PRN	Text file format
DIF	Data Interchange Format

* Excel can open files in this format, but not save them.

** When you open one of these files, Excel searches for the associated formatting file (either FMT or FM3) and attempts to translate the formatting.

Opening a Workbook File

Excel's primary file type is called a *workbook* file. When you open a workbook in Excel, the entire file is loaded into memory, and any changes that you make occur only in the copy that's in memory.

To open an existing workbook file:

1. Choose File⇨Open to bring up the Open dialog box.

You can also use any of the following methods to bring up the Open dialog box:

- Click the Open button on the Standard toolbar.

- Press Ctrl+O.

- Press Ctrl+F12 (or Alt+Ctrl+F2 if your keyboard lacks an F12 function key).

2. Specify the folder that contains the file.

You can select more than one file in the Open dialog box. The trick is to hold down the Ctrl key while you click on the filenames. After you select all of the files you want, click Open.

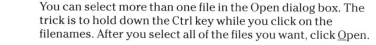

3. Select the workbook file and click Open or double-click the filename.

Other ways to open a workbook file:

+ Double-click the workbook icon in any folder window. If Excel is not running, it will be started automatically. Or you can drag a workbook icon into the Excel window to load the workbook.

+ Excel lists the last four files you've worked with at the bottom of the File menu. If the file you want appears in this list, you can choose it directly from the menu.

+ If you find that you use the same workbook every time you start Excel, you can make this workbook open automatically whenever Excel starts. Just move the workbook to the Excel\XLstart folder.

Protecting a Worksheet

Deleting a single formula on a worksheet often has a ripple effect, causing other formulas to produce an error value or, even worse, incorrect results. You can circumvent such problems by protecting your worksheets from being modified:

1. Choose the Tools⇨Protection⇨Protect Sheet command.

The Protect Sheet dialog box appears.

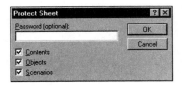

2. Choose the appropriate option or options and click OK.

Contents	Selecting this option prevents the cell from being changed.
Objects	Selecting this option prevents drawing objects (including embedded charts) from being changed.
Scenarios	Selecting this option prevents defined scenarios from being changed.

3. You have the option of providing a password in the Protect Sheet dialog box:

- If you enter a password, the password must be reentered before the sheet can be unprotected.

- If you don't supply a password, anyone can unprotect the sheet.

Remember: By default, all cells have their Locked property turned on. Before protecting a worksheet, you'll normally want to turn the Locked property off for input cells. You can change the Locked property of a cell or drawing object by accessing its Format dialog box and clicking the Protection tab. (For more information, see Chapter 6 of *Excel For Windows 95 For Dummies.*)

You can't change a cell's Locked property while the worksheet is protected. You must unprotect the sheet to make any changes and then protect it again. To remove protection from a protected sheet, choose the Tools⇨Protection⇨Unprotect Sheet command.

Protecting a Workbook File

Sometimes, you may want to protect a workbook's structure from being modified.

1. Choose the Tools⇨Protection⇨Protect Workbook command to display the dialog box shown below.

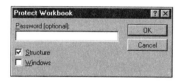

2. Choose the appropriate option and click OK.

Structure	Protects the workbook window from being moved or resized.
Windows	Prevents any of the following changes to a workbook: Adding a sheet, deleting a sheet, moving a sheet, renaming a sheet, hiding a sheet, or unhiding a sheet.

3. You can supply a password or not, depending on the level of protection you need.

To remove protection from a protected workbook, choose the Tools⇨Protection⇨Unprotect Workbook command.

Routing (Sending) a Workbook

Excel's routing feature lets you send a copy of a workbook to multiple members of a workgroup. After the routing is finished, the workbook is returned to you, complete with all the input from the others.

To route a workbook:

1. Choose the File⇨Add Routing Slip command or use the Routing Slip button on the WorkGroup toolbar.

Excel displays the Routing Slip dialog box.

2. Click the Address button to select the names of those who will receive the routed workbook.

3. Add a message in the Message Text field.

4. Select either sequential routing (One After Another) or simultaneous routing (All at Once) and click Add Slip.

TIP

See also "Mailing a Workbook File," in this part.

Saving a Workbook File

When you save the workbook, Excel saves the copy in memory to your disk — overwriting the previous copy of the file. To save the active workbook to disk:

1. Choose the File⇨Save command.

You may prefer to use any of the following methods to save:

- Click the Save button on the Standard toolbar
- Press the Ctrl+S shortcut key combination
- Press the Shift+F12 shortcut key combination

If the file has not been saved yet, Excel will prompt you for a name using its Save As dialog box.

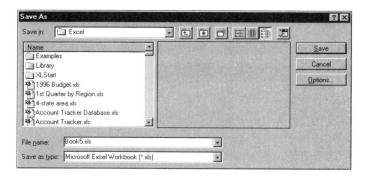

2. Select the folder that will hold the file.

3. Enter a name in the File name box. (A filename can consist of as many as 255 characters, including spaces.)

4. Click Save.

Remember: Be careful if you plan to share a worksheet file with someone who doesn't use Windows 95. Pre-95 versions of Windows don't support long filenames, so the filename may appear truncated.

You should save your work at a time interval that corresponds to the maximum amount of time that you're willing to lose. For example, if you don't mind losing an hour's work, save your file every hour. Most people save at more frequent intervals.

See also "Saving your work automatically," in this part.

Saving a workbook under a different name

Sometimes, you may want to keep multiple versions of your work by saving each successive version under a different name.

To save a workbook with a different name:

1. Use File⇨Save As to display the Save As dialog box.

2. Select the folder in which to store the workbook.

3. Enter a new filename in the File name box.

4. Click Save.

A new copy is created with a different name, but the original version of the file remains intact.

You can also use the File⇨Save As command to make a backup copy of a workbook simply by saving the file (with the same name) to a floppy disk, a different drive, or a different folder. Excel remembers the last place that it was saved, so you may want to save the workbook again in its original location.

Saving a workbook file in an older Excel format

Excel 5 and Excel for Windows 95 use the same file format, so file sharing usually presents no problems. However, if you send a workbook to someone who uses a pre-5.0 version of Excel, you must save the file in a format that the earlier version can read.

To save a workbook for an earlier version of Excel:

1. Choose the File⇨Save As command.

2. In the drop-down list box labeled Save as type, choose the format to save the file in.

3. Click Save.

Remember: Excel 5 was the first version to use multisheet workbooks. Prior to Excel 5, worksheets, chart sheets, and macro sheets were all stored in separate files. Consequently, if you share a multisheet workbook with someone who still uses one of these older versions, you must save each sheet separately — and in the proper format.

See also "Exporting a Text File," in this part.

Saving your work automatically

If you're the type who gets so wrapped up in your work that you forget to save your file on a regular basis, you may be interested in Excel's AutoSave feature. AutoSave automatically saves your workbooks at a pre-specified interval.

Using this feature requires that you load an add-in file that is included with Excel, but not normally installed. To install the AutoSave add-in:

1. Select Tools⇨Add-Ins to display the Add-Ins dialog box.

2. Click AutoSave in the list of add-ins and then click OK.

The add-in will be installed every time you run Excel. If you no longer want to use AutoSave, repeat the process and uncheck the AutoSave add-in.

![REMEMBER icon] After Autosave is installed, the Tools menu will have a new menu item: AutoSave. Selecting the Tools➪AutoSave command displays the AutoSave dialog box.

Using an Autotemplate

An *autotemplate* is a workbook that is used as the basis for a new workbook, a new worksheet, a new dialog sheet, or a new XLM macro sheet. Autotemplates are useful if you want to change the default settings for a new workbook or new sheets that are added to existing workbooks. Autotemplates are stored in your Excel\XLstart folder. An autotemplate workbook can have any of the following names:

✦ **Book.xlt:** A template for the new default workbook. This template can have any number of sheets, formatted as you like.

✦ **Sheet.xlt:** A template for a new worksheet added to an existing workbook. This should consist of a single worksheet.

✦ **Dialog.xlt:** A template for a new dialog sheet added to an existing workbook. This should consist of a single dialog sheet.

✦ **Macro.xlt:** A template for a new Excel 4.0 macros sheet added to a new workbook. (This option is for compatibility purposes and is not very useful.)

Using a Workspace File

Workspace means all of the workbooks and their screen positions and window sizes — sort of a snapshot of Excel's current state.

You may have a project that uses two or more workbooks, and you like to arrange the windows in a certain way to make it easy to access them. Fortunately, Excel lets you save your entire workspace to a file. Then, you can open the workspace file and Excel will be set up exactly as it was when you saved your workspace.

Opening a workspace file

Choose the File➪Open command to open a workspace file. Excel will open all of the workbooks that you originally saved.

Saving a workspace file

1. Choose the File➪Save Workspace command.

2. You can use the proposed name (Resume.xlw) or enter a different name in the File name field.

3. Click the Save button and the workspace will be saved to a disk.

A workspace file does not include the workbook files themselves — only the information needed to recreate the workspace. The workbooks are saved in standard workbook files. Therefore, if you distribute a workspace file to a coworker, make sure that you also include the workbook files that the workspace file refers to.

If you save your workspace file in the XLstart folder, Excel opens the workspace file automatically when it starts up.

Working with Worksheets

A workbook can consist of any number of worksheets. Each sheet has a tab that appears at the bottom of the workbook window. To activate a different sheet, just click its tab. If the tab for the sheet that you want to activate is not visible, use the tab scrolling buttons to scroll the sheet tabs.

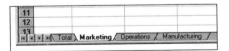

Remember: If a sheet is hidden, its tab will also be hidden. Before you can activate a hidden sheet, use the Format➪Sheet➪Unhide command to unhide it.

You also can use thse shortcut keys to activate a different sheet:

✦ **Ctrl+PgUp:** Activates the previous sheet, if there is one.

✦ **Ctrl+PgDn:** Activates the next sheet, if there is one.

Adding a new worksheet

There are three ways to add a new worksheet to a workbook:

✦ Select the Insert⇨Worksheet command.

✦ Right-click on a sheet tab, choose Insert from the shortcut menu, and select Worksheet from the Insert dialog box.

✦ Press Shift+F11.

Excel inserts a new worksheet before the active worksheet; the new worksheet then becomes the active worksheet.

To add worksheets after inserting a worksheet, press F4 (the shortcut for the Edit⇨Repeat command) or Ctrl+Y once for each sheet that you want to add.

You can add other types of sheets by choosing the appropriate command from the menu:

To add a new . . .	*Choose this command*
VBA module	Insert⇨Macro⇨Module
Dialog sheet	Insert⇨Macro⇨Dialog
Excel 4 macro sheet	Insert⇨Macro⇨MS Excel 4.0 Macro
Chart sheet	Insert⇨Chart⇨As New Sheet

Arranging windows automatically

If you want all of your unhidden workbook windows to be visible, you can move and resize them manually — or you can let Excel do it automatically.

Window⇨Arrange displays a dialog box that lists the four window arrangement options. Just select the one you want and click OK.

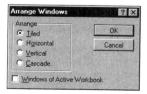

Changing a sheet's name

Worksheets, by default, are named Sheet1, Sheet2, and so on. Providing more meaningful names is usually a good idea. To change a sheet's name, use any of these methods:

+ Choose the Format⇨Sheet⇨Rename command.

+ Double-click on the sheet tab.

+ Right-click on the sheet tab and choose the Rename command from the shortcut menu.

Excel displays the Rename Sheet dialog box. Enter the new name and click OK. The sheet tab displays the new name.

Sheet names can be up to 31 characters, and spaces are allowed, but not the following characters: [] (square brackets); : (colon); / (slash); \ (backslash); ? (question mark); and * (asterisk).

Keep in mind that the name you give will be displayed on the tab; a longer name results in wider tabs. Therefore, if you use lengthy sheet names, you'll be able to see fewer sheet tabs without scrolling.

Changing a window's size (Maximizing, Minimizing, and Restoring)

A window in Excel can be in any of three states:

 + Maximized to fill the entire workspace. A maximized window does not have a title bar, and the workbook's name appears in Excel's title bar. To maximize a window, click on its Maximize button.

 + Minimized to appear as a small window with only a title bar. To minimize a Window, click on its Minimize button.

 + Restored to a non-maximized size. To restore a window, click on its Restore button.

You can also use the following key combinations:

Key Combination	Action
Ctrl+F5	Restores a window
Ctrl+F9	Minimizes a window
Ctrl+F10	Maximizes a window

When you maximize one window, all the other windows are maximized, too (but you can't see them).

Many users prefer to do most of their work with maximized workbook windows. This lets you see more cells and eliminates the distraction of other workbook windows getting in the way.

Copying a worksheet

You can make an exact copy of a worksheet — either in its original workbook or in a different workbook — in one of two ways:

✦ Select the Edit⇨Move or Copy Sheet command. Select the location for the copy and make sure that the check box labeled Create a Copy is checked.

✦ Click the sheet tab, press Ctrl, and drag it to its desired location. When you drag, the mouse pointer changes to a small sheet with a plus sign on it.

If necessary, Excel changes the name of the copied sheet to make it unique within the workbook.

Creating multiple windows (views) for a workbook

Sometimes, you may like to view two different parts of a worksheet at once. Or, you may want to examine more than one sheet in the same workbook. You can accomplish either of these actions by displaying your workbook in one or more additional windows.

To create a new view of the active workbooks choose Window⇨New Window. Excel displays a new window with the active workbook. To help you keep track of the windows, Excel appends a colon and a number to each window.

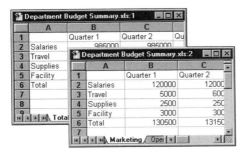

Remember: A single workbook can have as many views (that is, separate windows) as you like. Each window is independent of the others.

Displaying multiple windows for a workbook also makes it easier to copy information from one worksheet to another. You can use Excel's drag-and-drop procedures to copy a cell, a range, a graphic object, or a chart.

Creating named views

Excel lets you name various *views* of your worksheet and to switch quickly among these named views. A view includes settings for window size and position, frozen panes or titles, outlining, zoom factor, the active cell, print area, and many of the settings in the Options dialog box. A view can also include hidden print settings and hidden rows and columns.

The named views feature is an add-in that must be loaded. If the View⇨View Manager command isn't available, open the add-in:

1. Select the Tools⇨Add-Ins command.

2. Select the View Manager add-in from the list displayed in the Add-Ins dialog box.

If View Manager does not appear in the list, you'll need to run the Excel Setup program (or Microsoft Office Setup program) to add it.

After View Manager is loaded, you'll have access to a new command: View⇨View Manager. When you select this command, you get the View Manager dialog box.

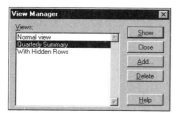

The View Manager dialog box displays a list of all named views:

✦ To use a particular view, select it from the list and click the Show button.

✦ To add a view, click the Add button and provide a name.

✦ To delete a named view from the list, click the Delete button.

Deleting a worksheet

You can delete a worksheet in one of two ways:

✦ Activate the sheet and select the Edit⇨Delete Sheet command.

✦ Right-click on the sheet tab and choose the Delete command from the shortcut menu.

In either case, Excel asks you to confirm the fact that you want to delete the sheet.

To select multiple sheets to delete, press Ctrl while clicking the sheet tabs that you want to delete. To select a group of contiguous sheets, click the first sheet tab, press Shift, and then click the last sheet tab.

When you delete a worksheet, it's gone for good. This is one of the few operations in Excel that can't be undone.

Freezing row or column titles

Many worksheets (such as budgets) are set up with row and column headings. When you scroll through such a worksheet, it's very easy to get lost when the row and column headings scroll out of view. Excel provides a handy solution: freezing rows and/or columns.

To freeze rows or columns:

1. Move the cell pointer to the cell below the row that you want to freeze and to the right of the column that you want to freeze.

2. Select the Window⇨Freeze Panes command.

Excel inserts dark lines to indicate the frozen rows and columns. These frozen rows and columns remain visible as you scroll throughout the worksheet.

To remove the frozen rows or columns, select the Window⇨Unfreeze Panes command.

See also "Splitting panes," in this part.

Hiding and unhiding a worksheet

Hiding a worksheet is useful if you don't want others to see it or if you just want to get it out of the way. When a sheet is hidden, its sheet tab is hidden also.

To hide a worksheet, choose the Format⇨Sheet⇨Hide command. The active worksheet (or selected worksheets) will be hidden from view.

Remember: Every workbook must have at least one visible sheet, so Excel won't allow you to hide all sheets in a workbook.

To unhide a hidden worksheet:

1. Choose the Format⇨Sheet⇨Unhide command.

A dialog box pops up listing all hidden sheets.

2. Choose the sheet that you want to unhide and click on OK.

If a VBA (Visual Basic for Applications) module is the active sheet, use the Edit⇨Sheet⇨Hide or Edit⇨Sheet⇨Unhide commands.

See also "Adding a new worksheet," in this part. You can even take a look at Chapter 12 in *Excel For Windows 95 For Dummies* for more information on VBA modules.

Moving a sheet

Sometimes, you want to rearrange the order of worksheets in a workbook — or move a sheet to a different workbook (to move a worksheet to a different workbook, both workbooks must be open).

First, select the sheet that you want to move by clicking on the sheet tab. You also can move multiple sheets at once by selecting them: Press Ctrl while you click the sheet tabs that you want to move.

There are two ways to move a selected worksheet(s):

✦ Select the Edit➪Move or Copy Sheet command. The Move or Copy dialog box pops up asking you to select the workbook and the new location.

✦ Click the sheet tab and drag it to its desired location (either in the same workbook or in a different workbook). When you drag, the mouse pointer changes to a small sheet and a small arrow guides you.

Dragging is usually the easiest method, but if the workbook has many sheets, you may prefer to use the Move or Copy dialog box.

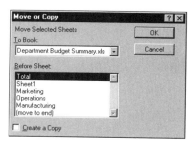

Remember: If you move a worksheet to a workbook that already has a sheet with the same name, Excel changes the name to make it unique. For example, Sheet1 becomes Sheet1 (2).

Moving and resizing windows

To move a window, first make sure that it is not maximized. If maximized, click its Restore button. Move the window by clicking and dragging its title bar with your mouse. Note that the window can extend off-screen in any direction, if you like.

To resize a window, click and drag any of its borders until it's the size you want it to be. When you position the mouse pointer on a window's border, the mouse pointer changes shape to let you know that you can then click and drag. To resize a window horizontally and vertically at the same time, click and drag any of its corners.

Although using a mouse to manipulate Excel's windows is usually the most efficient route, you also can perform these techniques using the keyboard.

Key Combination	Action
Ctrl+F4	Closes a window
Ctrl+F6	Activates the next window
Ctrl+Shift+F6	Activates the previous window
Ctrl+Tab	Activates the next window
Ctrl+Shift+Tab	Activates the previous window
Ctrl+F7	Moves a window*
Ctrl+F8	Resizes a window*
Alt+W[n]	Activates the nth window

* Use the direction keys to make the change and then press Enter.

Moving around in a worksheet

Navigating through a worksheet with a mouse works just as you would expect. Just click a cell and it becomes the active cell. If the cell that you want to activate is not visible in the workbook window, you can use the scroll bars to scroll the window in any direction.

♦ To scroll one cell, click one of the arrows on the scroll bar.

♦ To scroll by a complete screen, click either side of the scroll bar's "thumb" (the large center button).

♦ To scroll faster, drag the thumb.

Notice that only the active workbook window has scroll bars. When you activate a different window, the scroll bars appear.

Compared with the previous versions of Excel, the scroll bars work a little differently in Excel for Windows 95. When you drag the scroll bar's thumb, a small box appears that tells you which row or column you will scroll to when you release your finger from the mouse.

Remember: Using the scroll bars doesn't change the active cell. It simply scrolls the worksheet. To change the active cell, you must click on a new cell after scrolling.

The next table summarizes all of the worksheet movement keys available in Excel.

Key	Action
Up arrow	Moves the active cell up one row
Down arrow	Moves the active cell down one row
Left arrow	Moves the active cell one column to the left
Right arrow	Moves the active cell one column to the right
PgUp	Moves the active cell up one screen
PgDn	Moves the active cell down one screen
Alt+PgDn	Moves the active cell right one screen
Alt+PgUp	Moves the active cell left one screen
Ctrl+Backspace	Scrolls to display the active cell
Up arrow*	Scrolls the screen up one row (active cell does not change)
Down arrow*	Scrolls the screen down one row (active cell does not change)
Left arrow*	Scrolls the screen left one column (active cell does not change)
Right arrow*	Scrolls the screen right one column (active cell does not change)

* With Scroll Lock on

The actions for some of the keys in the preceding table may be different, depending on the transition options that you've set.

1. Select the Tools⇨Options command.

2. Click the Transition tab in the Options dialog box.

If the Transition Navigation Keys option is checked, the navigation keys correspond to those used in Lotus 1-2-3. Generally, it's better to use standard Excel navigation keys than those for 1-2-3.

Splitting panes

Splitting a window into two or four panes lets you view multiple parts of the same worksheet.

✦ The Window⇨Split command splits the active worksheet into two or four separate panes.

✦ The split occurs at the location of the cell pointer.

✦ You can use the mouse to drag the pane and resize it.

✦ To remove the split panes, choose Window⇨Remove Split.

A faster way to split and unsplit panes is to drag either the vertical or horizontal split bar, shown below. To remove split panes using the mouse, drag the pane separator all the way to the edge of the window or just double-click it.

	A	B	C	D	D
1					
2					
3					
4					
5					
6					
7					
8					
9					
10					

Book6

Sheet1

See also "Freezing row or column titles," in this part.

Zooming worksheets

Normally, everything you see in Excel is at 100 percent. You can change the "zoom percentage" from 10 percent (very tiny) to 400 percent (huge). Using a small zoom percentage can help you get a bird's-eye view of your worksheet to see how it's laid out. Zooming in is useful if your eyesight isn't quite what it used to be and you have trouble deciphering those 8-point sales figures.

The easiest way to change the zoom factor of the active worksheet is to use the Zoom Control on the Standard toolbar. Just click on the arrow and select the desired zoom factor. Your screen transforms immediately.

The Selection option in the toolbar Zoom Control drop-down list zooms the worksheet to display only the selected cells. This option is useful if you want to view only a particular range.

For finer control over the zoom factor, use the View⇨Zoom command. This command displays a dialog box that lets you enter a value between 10 and 400.

Remember: Zooming only affects the active worksheet. Also, the zoom factor affects only how the worksheet is displayed on-screen and not how it is printed. There are separate options for changing the size of your printed output (use the File⇨Page Setup command). For more information on printing options, see Chapter 5 in *Excel For Windows 95 For Dummies.*

Part III

Formatting, Outlining, and Printing Your Work

The end result of most spreadsheet work is the printed page that you can take to your boss for detailed data analysis. This part deals with topics related to formatting your work to get it ready for printing, creating outlines, and printing your worksheet.

In this part . . .

- ✓ Using different type fonts, sizes, and attributes
- ✓ Changing the way cell contents are aligned within cells
- ✓ Changing colors (and patterns) in your worksheet
- ✓ Adjusting row heights and column widths
- ✓ Adding borders around cells
- ✓ Changing the way numbers look
- ✓ Creating and using worksheet outlines
- ✓ Setting options for printing
- ✓ Previewing your work before you print it
- ✓ Printing worksheets

Formatting Cells and Ranges

You have lots of control over the appearance of information that you enter into a cell. Changing the appearance of cell contents is known as *formatting*. Excel provides three ways to format cells:

✦ **Toolbar buttons:** Common formatting commands are available on toolbar buttons on the Formatting toolbar.

✦ **Shortcut keys:** Some common formats can be applied by pressing shortcut key combinations. For example, Ctrl+B makes the text bold.

✦ **The Format Cells dialog box:** This multipanel dialog box provides all of the cell formatting commands. Click on one of the six tabs to access a particular panel in the dialog box.

You can bring up the Format Cells dialog box in any of three ways:

✦ Choose the Format⇨Cells command.

✦ Press Ctrl+1.

✦ Right-click on the selected cell or range of cells and choose Format Cells from the shortcut menu.

You can format cells before or after you enter information. For example, if you're entering a series of numbers, you can preformat the cells so the numbers will appear with commas and the desired number of decimal places.

Remember: Formatting does not affect the contents of your worksheet — only the way the text and values appear in the cell.

Adding borders to a cell or range

Borders often are used to "group" a range of similar cells or simply as a way to delineate rows or columns for aesthetic purposes.

To add borders around a cell or range:

1. Select the cell or range.

2. Choose the Format⇨Cells command (or press Ctrl+1).

3. Click the Border tab in the Format Cells dialog box.

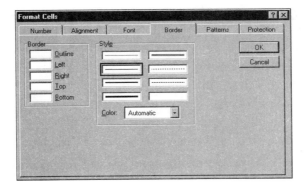

4. Select a line style from the Style portion of the dialog box.

5. Select the border position for the line style from the Border portion of the dialog box. Excel displays the selected border style in the dialog box. You can choose different styles for different border positions. You also can select a color for the border.

6. Click OK to apply the borders to your selection.

If you use border formatting in your worksheet, you may want to turn off the grid display to make the borders more pronounced. Use the View panel of the Options dialog box to do this.

Remember: Applying a border to the bottom of a cell is not the same as applying the underline attribute to the font. These two operations result in quite different effects.

See also "Changing text attributes," in this part.

Aligning cell contents

By default, cell contents appear at the bottom, numbers are right-aligned, text is left-aligned, and logical values are centered in cells.

You can apply the most common horizontal alignment options by selecting the cell or range of cells and using the tools on the Formatting toolbar: Align Left, Center, Align Right, and Center Across Columns.

You can use the following procedure to align cell contents:

1. Select the cell or range of cells to align.

2. Choose the Format⇨Cells command (or press Ctrl+1).

3. Click the Alignment tab in the Format Cells dialog box.

4. Select the desired horizontal or vertical alignment option.

5. Click OK.

Applying a background graphic

A new feature in Excel 95 lets you select a graphics file to serve as a background for a worksheet — similar to the *wallpaper* you may display on your Windows 95 desktop.

To add a background to a worksheet:

1. Activate the worksheet.

2. Choose the Format⇨Sheet⇨Background command. Excel displays a dialog box that lets you choose a graphics file.

3. Locate the desired graphics file (you may have to change to a different folder).

4. Click OK, and Excel tiles your worksheet with the graphic you selected.

In most cases, adding a graphic background will make it difficult to view text in cells, so you'll generally have to apply a background color to the non-empty cells. You'll probably want to turn off the gridline display because the gridlines show through the graphic.

Remember: The graphic background is for the screen display only; it doesn't get printed when you print the worksheet.

Applying background colors and patterns

To change the background color or pattern used in cells:

1. Select the cell or range that you want to format.

2. Choose the Format⇨Cells command (or press Ctrl+1).

3. Click the Patterns tab in the Format Cells dialog box.

4. Choose a color from the Cell Shading section.

5. To add a pattern, click the Pattern drop-down box and choose a pattern. If you like, you can choose a second color for the pattern.

6. Click OK to apply the color and/or pattern.

Remember: If you use background colors or patterns, printed output on a non-color printer may not produce the results you want.

See also "Printing colors in black and white," in this part.

A faster way to change the background color (but not a pattern) is to select the cells and then select a color from the Color tool on the Formatting toolbar.

Applying colors to text

The fastest way to change the color of text is:

1. Select the cell or range.

2. Select a color from the Font Color tool on the Formatting toolbar.

You can also change text color in the Font panel of the Format Cells dialog box.

Applying named styles

Excel lets you associate a named style with any cell. By default, all cells have the Normal style. In addition, Excel provides five other built-in styles — all of which control only the cell's number format. The styles available in every workbook are listed below.

Style Name	Description	Number Format Example
Normal	Excel's default style	1234
Comma*	Comma with two decimal places	1,234.00
Comma[0]	Comma with no decimal places	1,234
Currency*	Left-aligned dollar sign with two decimal places	$ 1,234.00
Currency[0]	Left-aligned dollar sign with no decimal places	$ 1,234
Percent*	Percent with no decimal places	12%

* This style can be applied by clicking a button on the Standard toolbar.

Excel also lets you create your own styles (for both numbers and text). To apply a custom style or a style that isn't associated with a toolbar button:

1. Select the cell or range that you want to apply the style to.

2. Choose Format➪Style. Excel displays its Style dialog box.

3. Select the style from the Style Name drop-down box.

4. Click OK to apply the style to the selection.

See also "Creating and modifying named styles," in this part.

Changing column width

You may want to change the width of a column if it's not wide enough to display values fully (you'll get a series of pound signs: ########), or simply to space out the cells horizontally. Before changing the width, you can select a number of columns so that the selected columns will all have the same width.

◆ Drag the right column border with the mouse until the column is the desired width.

◆ Choose the Format⇨Column⇨Width command and enter a value in the Column Width dialog box.

◆ Choose the Format⇨Column⇨AutoFit Selection command. This adjusts the width of the selected column(s) so that the widest entry in the column fits.

◆ Double-click on the right border of a column to automatically set the column width to the widest entry in the column.

To change the default width of all columns, use the Format⇨Column⇨Standard Width command. This displays a dialog box into which you enter the new default column width. All columns that haven't been previously adjusted take on the new column width.

Changing the default font (typeface)

If you would like to change the typeface used in all of the cells in a workbook, change the definition for the Normal style:

1. Select Format⇨Style. Excel displays its Style dialog box.

2. Select Normal from the drop-down list named Style Name.

3. Click the Modify button to display the Format Cells dialog box.

4. Click the Font tab in the Format Cells dialog box.

5. Select the font that you want to be the default.

6. Click OK twice. The font of all cells with the Normal style will be changed.

Remember: Changing the Normal style affects only the current workbook.

Changing fonts and text sizes

The easiest way to change the font or text size for selected cells is to use the Font and Font Size tools on the Formatting toolbar. Just select the cells, click on the appropriate tool, and select the font or size from the drop-down list.

You can also use the following technique, which lets you control several other properties of the font from a single dialog box:

1. Select the cell or range to modify.

2. Choose the Format⇨Cells command (or press Ctrl+1).

3. Click the Font tab in the Format Cells dialog box.

4. Make the desired changes and click OK.

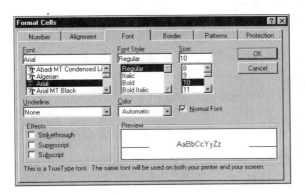

Notice that you also can change the font style (bold, italic), underlining, color, and effects (strikethrough, superscript, or subscript). If you click on the check box labeled <u>N</u>ormal Font, Excel displays the selections for the font defined for the Normal style.

See also "Creating and modifying named styles," in this part.

Changing row height

Row height is measured in points (a standard unit of measurement in the printing trade; 72 points equal one inch). Changing the row height is useful for spacing out rows; it's better to change the row height than to insert empty rows between rows of data. If you wish, you can select a number of rows before using these techniques to set row height:

✦ Drag the lower row border with the mouse until the row is the desired height.

✦ Choose the F<u>o</u>rmat⇨<u>R</u>ow⇨<u>H</u>eight command and enter a value (in points) in the Row Height dialog box.

✦ Double-click on the bottom border of a row to automatically set the row height to the tallest entry in the row. You also can use the F<u>o</u>rmat⇨<u>R</u>ow⇨<u>A</u>utoFit command for this.

Remember: The default row height depends on the font defined in the Normal style. Excel adjusts row heights automatically to accommodate the tallest font in the row. So, if you change the font size of a cell to, say, 20 points, Excel makes the row taller so that the entire text is visible.

See also "Creating and modifying named styles," in this part.

Changing text attributes

The easiest way to change text attributes (bold, italic, and underline) is to select the cell or range and then click the appropriate tool on the Formatting toolbar (Bold, Italic, or Underline).

Or, you can use the following shortcut keys to modify the selected cells.

Format	Shortcut Keys
Bold	Ctrl+B
Italic	Ctrl+I
<u>Underline</u>	Ctrl+U
~~Strikethrough~~	Ctrl+5

B These toolbar buttons and shortcut keys act as a toggle. For example, you can turn bold on and off by repeatedly pressing Ctrl+B (or clicking the Bold tool).

See also "Adding borders to a cell or range," in this part.

Changing text orientation (direction)

Normally, the contents of a cell are displayed horizontally. In some cases you may want to change the orientation (direction) of the text in a cell.

1. Select the cell or range to modify.

2. Choose the Format⇔Cells command (or press Ctrl+1).

3. Click the Alignment tab in the Format Cells dialog box.

4. Select one of the four options in the Orientation section.

5. Click OK to apply the formatting to the selection.

Remember: When using vertical orientation, you must increase the row height in order to display the text. Sometimes, it's preferable to use a text box to hold vertically oriented text because a text box is free floating and you don't have to increase the row height.

Copying formats

The quickest way to copy the formats from one cell to another cell or range is to use the Format Painter button on the Standard toolbar:

1. Select the cell or range that has the formatting attributes that you want to copy.

2. Click the Format Painter button. Notice that the mouse pointer appears as a miniature paintbrush.

3. Select (paint) the cells to which you want to apply the formats.

4. Release the mouse button, and the formats will be copied.

Double-clicking the Format Painter button causes the mouse pointer to remain a paintbrush after you release the mouse button. This lets you paint other areas of the worksheet with the same formats. To exit paint mode, click on the Format Painter button again (or press Esc).

Another way to copy formats:

1. Select the cell or range that has the formatting attributes that you want to copy.

2. Choose the Edit⇨Copy command.

3. Select the cell or range to which you want to apply the formats.

4. Choose the Edit⇨Paste Special command and click the Formats option.

Creating and modifying named styles

A named style can consist of settings for six different attributes. However, a style doesn't have to use *all* of the attributes. The attributes that make up a style are as follows:

✦ Number format

✦ Font (type, size, and color)

✦ Alignment (vertical and horizontal)

✦ Borders

✦ Pattern

✦ Protection (locked and hidden)

The easiest way to create a style is "by example." This means that you format a cell to have the style characteristics that you want, and then let Excel create the style from that cell. To create a style by example:

1. Select a cell and apply the formatting that will make up the style.

2. Choose the Format⇨Style command. Excel displays its Style dialog box.

3. Enter a name for the style in the Style Name drop-down box.

4. Remove the check marks from any of the six attributes that you don't want to be part of the style (optional).

5. Click OK to create the style.

The new style will be available and can be applied to other cells or ranges.

See also "Applying named styles," "Changing fonts and text sizes," and "Changing row height" in this part.

Creating custom number formats

Excel provides you with quite a few predefined number formats. If none of these is satisfactory, you'll need to create a custom number format.

1. Select the cell or range of cells that contains the values to format.

2. Choose the Format⇨Cells command (or press Ctrl+1).

3. Click the Number tab in the Format Cells dialog box.

4. Select the Custom category.

5. Construct a number format by specifying a series of codes in the Type field.

6. Click OK to store the custom number format and apply it to the selected cells.

The custom number format will then be available for use with other cells.

The formatting codes available for custom number formats, date, and time are described in Excel's online help.

Remember: Custom number formats are stored with the workbook. To make the custom format available in a different workbook, you must copy a cell that uses the custom format to the other workbook.

Formatting numbers

Excel is smart enough to perform some number formatting for you automatically. For example, if you enter **9.6%** into a cell, Excel knows that you want to use a percentage format and applies it for you automatically. Similarly, if you use commas to separate thousands (such as **123,456**), Excel applies comma formatting for you.

Use the Formatting toolbar to quickly apply common number formats. When you click on one of these buttons, the active cell takes on the specified number format. The table below lists these toolbar buttons.

	Button Name	*Formatting Applied*
$	Currency Style	Adds a dollar sign to the left, separates thousands with a comma, and displays the value with two digits to the right of the decimal point
%	Percent Style	Displays the value as a percentage with no decimal places
,	Comma Style	Separates thousands with a comma and displays the value with two digits to the right of the decimal place
+.0 .00	Increase Decimal	Increases the number of digits to the right of the decimal point by one
.00 +.0	Decrease Decimal	Decreases the number of digits to the right of the decimal point by one

Remember: These five toolbar buttons actually apply predefined *styles* to the selected cells.

If none of the predefined number formats fits the bill, you need to use the Format Cells dialog box:

1. Select the cell or range that contains the values to format.

2. Choose the F̲ormat⇨C̲ells command (or press Ctrl+1).

3. Click the Number tab.

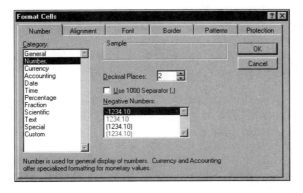

4. Select one of the 12 categories of number formats. When you select a category from the list box, the right side of the panel changes to display appropriate options.

5. Select an option from the right side of the dialog box. Options will vary, depending on your category choice. The top of the panel displays a sample of how the active cell will appear with the selected number format.

6. After you make your choices, click on OK to apply the number format to all of the selected cells.

Remember: If the cell displays a series of pound signs (such as #########), it means that the column is not wide enough to display the value using the number format that you selected. The solution is to make the column wider or change the number format.

Formatting selected characters in a cell

If a cell contains text, Excel lets you format individual characters in the cell. For example, you can make the first letter of the cell appear in a larger typeface (font).

To format only part of a cell:

1. Select the cell that you want to format.

2. Get into cell edit mode (press F2, or click the format bar).

3. Select the characters that you want to format. You can select characters by dragging the mouse over them or by holding down Shift as you press the left- or right-arrow key.

4. Use any of the standard formatting techniques: toolbar buttons, the Format Cells dialog box, or shortcut keys.

5. Press Enter.

The changes will apply only to the selected characters in the cell.

Remember: This technique works only with cells that contain text — it doesn't work with cells that contain values or formulas.

TIP If you want to apply character formatting to a value, format the value as Text using the Number panel of the Format Cells dialog box. Then you can apply individual character formatting to the cell contents.

Hiding cells

There are several ways to "hide" the contents of a cell:

✦ Apply a custom number format consisting of three semicolons (;;;).

✦ Make the text color the same as the background color.

✦ Add a rectangular object to the worksheet to cover the cells you want to hide.

All three of these techniques have the same flaw: When the cell pointer is on the cell, its contents can be seen in the formula bar. If you want to avoid this and make the cell contents truly invisible:

1. Select the cell or range.

2. Choose Format⇨Cells (or press Ctrl+1).

3. Click the Protection tab.

4. Check the Hidden check box.

5. Click OK.

6. Select the Tools⇨Protection⇨Protect Sheet command to turn on the Hidden attribute for the selected cells.

See also "Protecting a Worksheet," in Part II.

Remember: You won't be able to make any changes when the worksheet is protected.

Hiding columns and rows

Hiding columns and rows is useful if you don't want users to see particular information or if you don't want some information to be printed.

To hide a column(s) or row(s):

1. Select the column(s) or row(s) that you want to hide.

2. Choose Format⇨Column⇨Hide or Format⇨Row⇨Hide.

You also can drag a column's right border to the left or a row's bottom border upward to hide it.

Remember: A hidden column or row has a width or height of 0. When you use the arrow keys to move the cell pointer, cells in hidden columns or rows are skipped. In other words, you can't use the arrow keys to move to a cell in a hidden row or column.

See also "Unhiding rows or columns," in this part.

Justifying (refitting) text across cells

Justifying text redistributes the text in the cells so that it fits into a specified range. You can make the text either wider (so it uses fewer rows) or narrower (so that it uses more rows).

The figure below shows a range of text before and after being redistributed to fit a specified range.

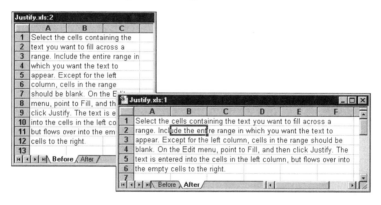

To justify text across cells:

1. Select the text to be justified. The text must be in cells in a single column. Blank rows serve as paragraph markers.

2. Extend the selection to the right so that the selection is as wide as you want the end result to be.

3. Choose the Edit⇨Fill⇨Justify command.

Excel redistributes the text, so that it fits in the selected range.

If the range you select isn't large enough to hold all of the text, Excel warns you and allows you to continue or abort. Be careful, because justified text overwrites anything that gets in its way.

Remember: In all cases, the text must be in a single column of cells. After you justify the text, it remains in a single column.

Unhiding rows or columns

Unhiding a hidden row or column can be a bit tricky because you can't directly select a row or column that's hidden. Here's how:

1. Choose Edit⇨Go To (or its F5 equivalent). Excel displays its Go To dialog box.

2. In the Reference field, enter a cell address that's in the hidden row or column. For example, if you want to unhide row 1, enter A1 (or any other cell address in row 1).

3. Choose the Format⇨Row⇨Unhide command or the Format⇨Column⇨Unhide command.

See also "Hiding columns and rows," in this part.

Using autoformats

Excel's AutoFormatting feature applies attractive formatting to a table automatically.

To apply an AutoFormat:

1. Move the cell pointer anywhere within a table that you want to format (Excel determines the table's boundaries automatically).

2. Choose the Format⇨AutoFormat command. Excel responds with its AutoFormat dialog box.

3. Select one of the 17 AutoFormats from the list and click OK. Excel formats the table using the selected AutoFormat.

You can't define your own AutoFormats, but you *can* control the type of formatting that is applied. When you click on the Options button in the AutoFormat dialog box, the dialog box expands to show six options.

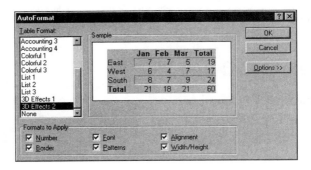

Initially, the six check boxes are all checked, which means that Excel will apply formatting from all six categories. If you would like it to skip one or more categories, just uncheck the appropriate boxes by clicking in them before you click OK.

Wrapping text within a cell

Wrapping text within a cell is a good way to display more information without making the column wider. This is useful for lengthy table headings, as shown below.

	A	B	C	D	E
1					
2		Projected Sales	Actual Sales	Actual minus Projected	
3	Chairs	244	211	-33	
4	Tables	45	55	10	
5	Desks	17	15	-2	
6	Lamps	24	30	6	
7		330	311	-19	
8					
9					

To format a cell or range so that the words wrap around:

1. Select the cell or range that you want to apply word wrap formatting to.

2. Choose Format➪Cells (or press Ctrl+1).

3. Click the Alignment tab of the Format Cells dialog box.

4. Check the box labeled Wrap Text.

5. Click OK to apply the formatting to the selection.

Remember: When you decrease the column width of a cell that's formatted with wrap text, the words will wrap around to the next line to accommodate the new column width.

Worksheet Outlining

Some types of worksheets may benefit from an outline. An outline lets you display hierarchical information at different levels of detail.

Creating an outline automatically

In most cases, the best approach is to let Excel create the outline for you. Excel can do the job in a few seconds, whereas you may take ten minutes or more.

To have Excel create an outline:

1. Move the cell pointer anywhere within the range of data that you're outlining.

2. Choose <u>D</u>ata⇨<u>G</u>roup and Outline⇨<u>A</u>uto Outline.

Excel analyzes the formulas in the range and creates the outline. Depending on the formulas you have, Excel creates a row outline, a column outline, or both.

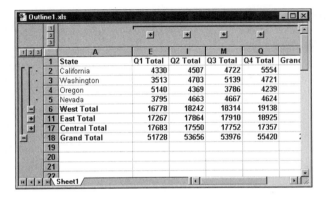

Remember: A worksheet can have only one outline. If the worksheet already has an outline, you'll be asked whether you want to modify the existing outline. Click on Yes to force Excel to remove the old outline and create a new one.

See also "Determining if a worksheet is suitable for an outline," in this part.

Creating an outline manually

Usually, letting Excel create the outline is the best approach. If the outline that Excel creates isn't what you had in mind, however, you can create one manually.

You must create an outline manually when:

✦ The summary rows aren't consistent (some formulas are above the data and some are below the data).

✦ The range doesn't contain any formulas. Because Excel uses the formulas to determine how to create the outline, it would not be able to make an outline if there were no formulas.

Creating an outline manually consists of creating groups of rows (for row outlines) or groups of columns (for column outlines).

To create a group of rows:

1. Select the entire row or rows that you want to be included in the group — but do *not* select the row that has the summary formulas.

2. Choose Data➪Group and Outline➪Group. Excel displays the outline symbols for the group as it's created.

3. Repeat Steps 1 and 2 for each group that you want to create.

When you collapse the outline (that is, show less detail), rows in the group will be hidden. But the summary row, which is not in the group, won't be hidden.

Follow the same steps to create a group of columns — but select columns instead of rows.

If you group the wrong rows or columns, you can ungroup the group with the Data➪Group and Outline➪Ungroup command.

Remember: You also can select groups of groups to create multilevel outlines. When creating multilevel outlines, always start with the "innermost" groupings and then work your way out.

See also "Determining if a worksheet is suitable for an outline," in this part.

Determining if a worksheet is suitable for an outline

Before you create an outline, you need to ensure that:

✦ The data is appropriate for an outline.

✦ The formulas are set up properly.

Generally, the data should be arranged in a hierarchy. An example of hierarchical data is a budget that consists of an arrangement such as the following:

Division

Department

Budget Category

Budget Item

In this case, each budget item (for example, airfare and hotel expenses) is part of a budget category (for example, travel expenses). Each department has its own budget, and the departments are rolled up into divisions. This type of arrangement is well-suited for a row outline.

Before creating an outline, make sure that the summary formulas are entered in the same relative location. Generally, formulas that compute summary formulas (such as subtotals) are entered below the data to which they refer. In some cases, however, the summary formulas are entered above the referenced cells.

If your summary formulas aren't consistent (that is, some are above and some are below the data), automatic outlining won't produce the results you want. You still can create an outline, but you must do it manually.

See also "Creating an outline automatically" and "Creating an outline manually," both in this part.

Expanding and contracting an outline

To display various levels of detail in a worksheet outline, click on the appropriate outline symbol at the left side of the screen (for row outlines) or the top of the screen (for column outlines).

Number symbols (1, 2, and so on)	Displays a level corresponding to the number. Clicking on the 1 button collapses the outline as small as it will go (less detail). Clicking on the 2 button expands it to show one level of detail, and so on. Choosing a level number displays the detail for that level, plus any lower levels. To display all of the detail, click on the highest level number.
Plus (+) or minus (-) symbols	Expands (+) or collapses (-) a particular section of the outline.

If you prefer, you can use the Hide Detail and Show Detail commands on the Data➪Group and Outline menu to hide and show details.

If you find yourself constantly adjusting the outline to show different reports, consider using the View Manager add-in. The View Manager lets you save a particular view and give it a name.

Hiding outline symbols

The symbols displayed when a worksheet outline is present can take up quite a bit of screen space. If you want to see as much of the data as possible on-screen, you can temporarily hide these symbols without removing the outline. To do so, press Ctrl+8.

Remember: When you hide the outline symbols, the outline is still in effect and the worksheet displays the data at the current outline level. That is, some rows or columns may be hidden.

If you use the View Manager to save named views of your outline, the status of the outline symbols is also saved as part of the view. This lets you name some views with the outline symbols and other views without them.

Removing an outline

If you decide that you no longer need an outline, you can remove it (the data will remain, but the outline will go away). Just select the Data⇨Group and Outline⇨Clear Outline command. The outline is fully expanded (all hidden rows and columns are unhidden), and the outline symbols disappear.

Removing an outline can't be undone, so make sure that you really want to remove the outline before selecting this command.

Printing Your Work

Clicking the Print button on the Standard toolbar is a quick way to print the current worksheet using the default settings. If you've changed any of the default print settings, Excel uses the settings you put in; otherwise, it uses these default settings:

- ✦ Prints the active worksheet (or all selected worksheets), including any embedded charts or drawing objects

- ✦ Prints one copy

- ✦ Prints the entire worksheet

- ✦ Prints in portrait mode

- ✦ Doesn't scale the printed output

- ✦ Uses 1-inch margins for the top and bottom and .75-inch margins for the left and right

- ✦ Prints the sheet name as a header on each page and puts page numbers in the footer of each page

- ✦ For wide worksheets that span multiple pages it prints down and then across

If you need to make many copies, it's usually more efficient to print one copy and use a photocopy machine.

Adjusting margins

A margin is the blank space on the side of the page. The wider the margins, the less space is available for printing. You can control all four page margins from Excel.

To adjust margins:

1. Select the File⇔Page Setup command.

2. Click the Margins tab in the Page Setup dialog box.

3. Click the appropriate spinner to change the margin value (or you can enter a value directly).

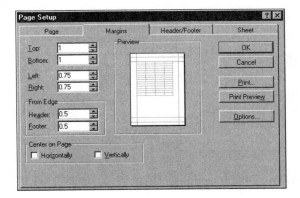

In addition to the page margins, you can adjust the distance of the header from the top of the page and the distance of the footer from the bottom of the page. These settings should be less than the corresponding margin; otherwise, the header or footer may overlap with the printed output.

You also can change the margins while you're previewing your output — ideal for last-minute adjustments before printing.

See also "Previewing your work," in this part.

Remember: The Preview box in the Page Setup dialog box is a bit deceiving because it doesn't really show you how your changes look in relation to the page. Rather, it simply displays a darker line to let you know which of the margins you're adjusting.

Centering printed output

Normally, Excel prints a page at the top and left margins. If you would like the output to be centered vertically or horizontally on the page:

1. Select the File⇨Page Setup command.

2. Click the Margins tab of the Page Setup dialog box.

3. Check the appropriate check boxes in the Center on Page section: Horizontally or Vertically.

Changing default printing settings with a template

If you find that you're never satisfied with Excel's default print settings, you may want to create a template with the print settings that you use most often.

1. Start with an empty workbook.

2. Adjust the print settings to your liking.

3. Save the workbook as a template in your Templates folder, using the name **Book.xlt**.

Excel will use this template as the basis for all new workbooks, and your custom print settings will be the default settings.

Changing the header or footer

A header is a line of information that appears at the top of each printed page. A footer is a line of information that appears at the bottom of each printed page.

Headers and footers each have three sections: left, center, and right. For example, you can specify a header that consists of your name left-justified, the worksheet name centered, and the page number right-justified.

To specify a header or footer:

1. Select the File⇨Page Setup command.

2. Click the Header/Footer tab of the Page Setup dialog box.

3. Select a pre-defined header or footer from the Header or Footer drop-down list.

If none of the pre-defined headers or footers is what you want, you'll need to define a customized header or footer:

1. Click the Custom Header or Custom Footer button in the Header/ Footer tab of the Page Setup dialog box. Excel displays a new dialog box.

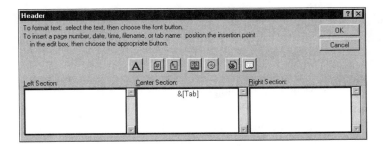

2. Enter the desired information in any or all of the three sections. Or, click any of the seven buttons (described below) to enter a special code.

Button	Code	Function
Font	Not applicable	Lets you choose a font for the selected text.
Page Number	&[Page]	Inserts the page number
Total Pages	&[Pages]	Inserts the total number of pages to be printed
Date	&[Date]	Inserts the current date
Time	&[Time]	Inserts the current time
File	&[File]	Inserts the workbook name
Sheet	&[Tab]	Inserts the sheet's name

3. Click OK.

You can combine text and codes and insert as many codes as you like into each section. If the text you enter uses an ampersand (&), you must enter it twice (because an ampersand is used by Excel to signal a code). For example, to enter the text *Research & Development* into a section of a header or footer, enter **Research && Development.**

You can use as many lines as you like. Use Alt+Enter to force a line break for multiline headers or footers.

Changing page orientation

To change the page orientation (landscape or portrait) of your printed output:

1. Select the File⇨Page Setup command.

2. Click the Page tab of the Page Setup dialog box.

3. Select either Portrait (tall pages) or Landscape (wide pages).

> Use landscape orientation if you have a wide range that doesn't fit on a vertically oriented page.

Faxing from Excel

If you have a fax board installed in your system, you can fax a worksheet to someone. The process works just like printing — but you have to select the fax as your printer in the Print dialog box.

1. Select the File➪Print command.

2. In the Print dialog box, select the fax device from the drop-down list labeled Printer Name (the exact name will vary).

3. Print your worksheet as usual. Instead of going to the printer, the worksheet will be faxed to the recipient whom you specify.

Remember: The procedure for specifying the fax's recipient varies depending on your fax software.

Excel remembers the last "printer" you selected, so when you want to print normally, make sure that you select a printer (not a fax).

Inserting manual page breaks

Excel handles page breaks automatically. After you print or preview your worksheet, it displays dashed lines to indicate where page breaks will occur. Sometimes, you want to force a page break — either a vertical or a horizontal one.

To insert a vertical manual page break:

1. Move the cell pointer to the cell that will begin the new page, but make sure that it's in column A (otherwise, you'll insert a vertical page break and a horizontal page break).

2. Choose Insert➪Page Break to create the page break.

To insert a horizontal page break:

1. Move the cell pointer to the cell that will begin the new page, but make sure that it's in row 1 (otherwise, you'll insert a horizontal page break and a vertical page break).

2. Select Insert➪Page Break to create the page break.

> When manipulating page breaks, it's often helpful to use the zoom feature to zoom out. This gives you a bird's-eye view of the worksheet and you can see more pages at once.

Previewing your work

Excel's print preview feature shows an image of the printed output on your screen — a handy feature that saves time and paper.

There are several ways to access the print preview feature:

✦ Select the File⇨Print Preview command.

✦ Click the Print Preview button on the Standard toolbar. Or, you can press Shift and click on the Print button on the Standard toolbar (the Print button serves a dual purpose).

✦ Click the Preview button in the Print dialog box.

✦ Click the Print Preview button in the Page Setup dialog box.

Any of these methods changes Excel's window to a special preview window, as shown in the following figure.

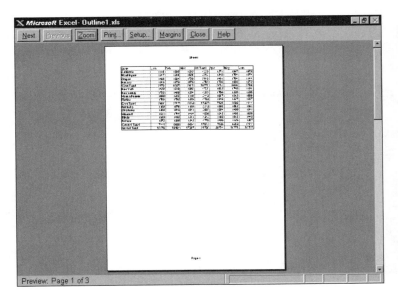

The preview window has several buttons along the top, the most important of which is Margins. Clicking it displays adjustable columns and margins. You can drag the column or margin markers to make changes that appear on-screen.

Remember: When you make changes to the column widths in the preview window, these changes also are made to your worksheet. Similarly, changing the margins in the preview window changes the settings that appear in the Margins panel of the Page Setup dialog box.

See also "Adjusting Margins," in this part.

Printing cell notes

If one or more cells in your worksheet has a cell note, you can print these notes along with the worksheet:

1. Select File⇨Page Setup.

2. Click the Sheet tab in the Page Setup dialog box.

3. Place a check next to the Notes check box.

Excel doesn't print the cell reference to which each note refers. Therefore, you may want to include the cell address in your note so you can tell which note goes with each cell.

Printing colors in black and white

If you have a colorful worksheet, but your printer is stuck in a monochrome world, you may discover that the worksheet colors don't translate well to black and white. In this case, you need to instruct Excel to ignore the colors when printing:

1. Select File⇨Page Setup.

2. Click the Sheet tab of the Page Setup dialog box.

3. Place a check next to the Black and White check box.

See also "Applying background colors and patterns," in this part.

Printing in draft quality

Printing in draft mode doesn't print embedded charts or drawing objects, cell gridlines, or borders. This usually reduces the printing time and is handy for getting a quick printout.

To print your work in draft mode:

1. Select File⇨Page Setup.

2. Click the Sheet tab of the Page Setup dialog box.

3. Place a check next to the Draft Quality check box.

Printing noncontiguous ranges

Excel lets you specify a print area that consists of noncontiguous ranges (a multiple selection). To do so:

1. Press Ctrl while you select the ranges.

2. Choose File⇨Print.

3. Select the Selection option.

This is a handy feature, but you may not like the fact that Excel prints each range beginning on a new sheet of paper.

One solution to this problem is to create live "snapshots" of the ranges and paste these snapshots to an empty area of the worksheet. Then you can print this new area that consists of the snapshots, and Excel won't skip to a new page for each range.

To create a live snapshot of a range:

1. Select the range and copy it to the Clipboard.

2. Activate the cell where you want to paste the snapshot (an empty worksheet is a good choice).

3. Press the Shift key and choose Edit⇨Paste Picture Link to paste a live link.

4. Repeat Steps 1 through 3 for the other ranges you want to print.

5. Select the range that holds the snapshot and print only that range.

After you've pasted them, you can rearrange the snapshots any way you like.

Remember: The pasted objects are truly live links: change a cell in the original range and the change appears in the linked picture.

Remember: The Edit⇨Paste Picture Link command is available only if you press Shift while you click on the Edit menu.

Printing or suppressing gridlines

To change the way Excel handles worksheet gridlines when printing:

1. Select the File⇨Page Setup command.

2. Click the Sheet tab of the Page Setup dialog box.

3. Place a check next to the Gridlines check box to print gridlines; remove the check to suppress gridline printing.

Remember: If you turned off the gridline display in the worksheet (in the View panel of the Options dialog box), Excel unchecks this box for you automatically. In other words, the default setting for this option is determined by the gridline display in your worksheet.

Printing row and column headings

If you want to make it easy to identify specific cells from a printout, you'll want to print the row and column headings. To do so:

1. Select the File⇨Page Setup command.

2. Click the Sheet tab of the Page Setup dialog box.

3. Place a check next to the Row and Column Headings check box.

Printing selected pages

If your printed output uses multiple pages, you may not always want to print all of the pages. To select a range of pages to print:

1. Select the File⇨Print command.

2. In the Page Range section of the Print dialog box, indicate the number of the first and last pages to print. You can use the spinner controls or type the page numbers in the edit boxes.

Removing manual page breaks

To remove a manual page break:

1. Move the cell pointer anywhere in the first row beneath the page break or the first column following a horizontal page break.

2. Select the Insert⇨Remove Page Break command.

To remove all manual page breaks in the worksheet, click on the Select All button (or press Ctrl+A); then choose the Insert⇨Remove Page Break command.

Scaling your printed output

Sometimes you may need your printed output to fit exactly on one page. Or, you may just want the worksheet to print smaller or larger than normal. Excel lets you scale the output from 10 percent to 400 percent of normal.

To scale your printed output:

1. Select File⇨Page Setup.

2. Click the Page tab of the Page Setup dialog box.

3. Enter a scaling factor manually in the % Normal Size box, or let Excel scale the output automatically to fit on the desired number of pages.

If you want to return to normal scaling, enter 100 in the box labeled % Normal Size.

Remember: Scaling printed output does not affect the zoom factor of the worksheet.

Selecting a printer

If you have access to more than one printer, you may need to select the correct printer before printing. To do so:

1. Select the File⇨Print command.

2. In the Print dialog box, select the printer from the drop-down list labeled Printer Name.

The Print dialog box also lists information about the selected printer, such as its status and where it's connected.

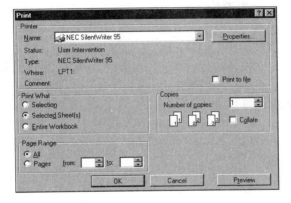

Clicking on the Properties button displays a property box for the selected printer. The exact dialog box that you see depends on the printer. This lets you adjust printer-specific settings. In most cases, you won't have to change any of these settings, but it's a good idea to be familiar with the settings that you can change.

Selecting paper size

To change the paper size of the printed output:

1. Select the File⇨Page Setup command.

2. Click the Page tab of the Page Setup dialog box.

3. Select the paper size from the list labeled Paper Size.

Remember: Your printer must be capable of printing the selected size — and you must have paper of that size loaded.

Setting the print area

To specify a particular range to print:

1. Select the range that you want to print.

2. Choose the File⇨Print Area⇨Set Print Area Command.

Another way to print only a specific range is:

1. Select a range of cells.

2. Choose the File⇨Print command.

3. Choose the Selection option in the Print dialog box.

Setting print titles

Many worksheets are set up with titles in the first row and descriptive names in the first column. If such a worksheet requires more than one page to print, you may find it difficult to read subsequent pages because the text in the first row and first column won't be printed. Excel offers a simple solution: print titles.

To specify print titles:

1. Select the File⇨Page Setup command.

2. Click the Sheet tab of the Page Setup dialog box.

3. Activate the appropriate box in the Print Titles section and select the rows or columns in the worksheet. Or, you can enter these references manually. For example, to specify rows 1 and 2 as repeating rows, enter **1:2**.

Remember: Don't confuse print titles with headers; these are two different concepts. Headers appear at the top of each page and contain information such as the worksheet name, date, or page number. Print titles describe the data being printed, such as field names in a database table or list.

You can specify different print titles for each worksheet in the workbook. Excel remembers print titles by creating sheet-level names (Print_Titles).

Specifying the beginning page number

If your printed output will be inserted into another report, you may want to specify a beginning page number so the pages will be collated correctly when inserted into the report. To do so:

1. Select the File⇨Page Setup command.

2. Click the Page tab of the Page Setup dialog box.

3. Specify a page number for the first page.

Remember: You specify page numbers in the header or footer. If you're not printing page numbers in your header or footer, this setting is irrelevant.

Specifying what to print

Excel gives you several options as to what to print.

1. Select the File⇨Print command.

2. In the Print What section of the Print dialog box, specify what to print. You have three options:

- **Selection:** Prints only the range that you selected before issuing the File⇨Print command.

- **Selected Sheet(s):** Prints the active sheet or all sheets that you selected. You can select multiple sheets by pressing Ctrl and clicking on the sheet tabs. If multiple sheets are selected, each sheet begins printing on a new page.

- **Entire Workbook:** Prints the entire workbook, including chart sheets, dialog sheets, and VBA modules.

Remember: If you choose the Selected Sheet(s) option, Excel prints the entire sheet — or just the range named Print_Area. Each worksheet can have a range named Print_Area. You can set the print area by selecting it and then choosing the File⇨Print Area⇨Set Print Area command. This is a standard named range, so you can edit the range's reference manually if you like.

Spell checking

Excel has a spell checker that works just like the feature found in word processing programs.

You can access the spell checker using any of these methods:

✦ Select the Tools⇨Spelling command.

✦ Click the Spelling button on the Standard toolbar.

✦ Press F7.

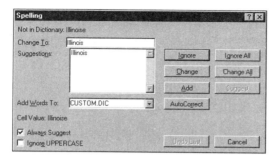

The extent of the spell checking depends on what was selected when you accessed the dialog box.

What Is Selected	What Gets Checked
A single cell	The entire worksheet, including cell contents, notes, text in graphic objects and charts, and page headers and footers.
A range of cells	Only that range is checked.
A group of characters in the formula bar	Only those characters are checked.

If Excel encounters a word that isn't in the current dictionary or is misspelled, it offers a list of suggestions you can click on to respond to.

Part IV

Entering and Editing Worksheet Data

This part deals with two general topics: entering data into worksheet cells and editing (or changing) the data after it has been entered. Entering formulas is covered in Part V.

In this part . . .

✔ Entering data into cells

✔ Selecting cells and ranges

✔ Copying cells and ranges

✔ Editing the contents of a cell

✔ Moving cells and ranges

✔ Erasing cells and ranges

✔ Searching and replacing data

✔ Undoing changes and mistakes

Copying Cells and Ranges

Often, you'll want to copy the contents of a cell to another cell or range. Copying is a very common spreadsheet operation, and several types of copying are allowed. You can

+ Copy one cell to another cell.

+ Copy a cell to a range of cells. The source cell is copied to every cell in the destination range.

+ Copy a range to another range. Both ranges are the same size.

Remember: Copying a cell normally copies the cell contents, its cell note (if any), and the formatting that was applied to the original cell. When you copy a cell that contains a formula, the cell references in the copied formulas are changed automatically to be relative to their new destination.

See also "Using Cell Notes," in this part.

In general, copying consists of two steps:

1. Select the cell or range to copy (the source range) and copy it to the Windows Clipboard.

2. Move the cell pointer to the range that will hold the copy (the destination range) and paste the Clipboard contents.

Copying a cell to another cell or a range

To copy the contents of one cell to a range of cells

1. Move the cell pointer to the cell to copy.

2. Click the Copy button on the Standard toolbar (you can also press Ctrl+C or choose Edit⇨Copy.

3. Select the cell or range that will hold the copy.

4. Press Enter.

If the range that you're copying to is adjacent to the cell that you're copying from, you can drag the cell's AutoFill handle to copy it to the adjacent range.

If the location that you're copying to isn't too far away, you can

1. Move the cell pointer to the cell to copy.

2. Hold down the Ctrl key.

3. Move the mouse pointer to any of the cell's borders. The mouse pointer displays a small plus sign (+).

4. Drag the mouse to the location where you want to copy the cell or range.

5. Release the mouse button.

Excel copies the cell or range to the new location.

Copying a range to another range

To copy the contents of one range to another range of the same size

1. Select the range to copy.

2. Choose the Edit⇔Copy command (you can also press Ctrl+C or click the Copy button on the Standard toolbar).

3. Select the upper-left cell of the range that will hold the copy.

4. Press Enter.

Copying data as a picture

In some situations, you may want to copy a cell or range as a picture. Doing so creates a graphic object that's a mirror image of the copied range.

To copy data as a picture

1. Select the cell or range.

2. Choose the Edit⇔Copy command (you can also press Ctrl+C or click the Copy button on the Standard toolbar).

3. Activate the cell where you want to paste the picture.

4. Press the Shift key and choose the Edit⇔Paste Picture command.

This procedure pastes a picture of the original cell or range. If you would like the picture to be linked to the cell, Press the Shift key and choose the Edit⇔Paste Picture Link command in Step 4. With a linked picture, any changes you make to the source range also appear in the picture.

Remember: The Edit⇔Paste Link and the Edit⇔Paste Picture Link commands are available only if you press Shift while you click on the Edit menu.

Copying data to another worksheet or workbook

To copy the contents of a cell or range to another worksheet or workbook

1. Select the cell or range to copy.

2. Choose the Edit⇨Copy command (you can also press Ctrl+C or click the Copy button on the Standard toolbar).

3. Click the tab of the worksheet that you're copying to.

If the worksheet is in a different workbook, activate that workbook and then click the tab of the worksheet that will hold the copied data.

4. Select the upper-left cell of the range that will hold the copy.

5. Press Enter.

Copying formulas as values

Sometimes you may want to convert a formula to its current value:

1. Select the cell that contains the formula.

If you want to convert several formulas you can select a range.

2. Click the Copy button on the Standard toolbar (you can also press Ctrl+C or choose Edit⇨Copy.

3. Choose the Edit⇨Paste Special command.

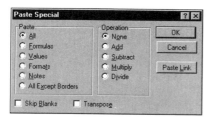

4. In the Paste Special dialog box, select the Values option button.

5. Click OK.

6. Press Enter to cancel Copy mode.

Remember: The procedure above overwrites the formulas. If you want to put the current values of the formulas in a different area of the worksheet, select a different (blank) range before Step 3, above.

Dragging a Range to the Desktop

Excel 95 has a new feature that lets you drag a selected range to the Windows desktop. The official name for this copied range is a *scrap*.

The scrap appears as an icon (picture) that you can use at a later time. For example, you can drag the scrap to another worksheet or to another application. When you drag a scrap to another worksheet, it creates an embedded OLE object.

See also topics concerning embedding in Part VIII.

To drag a scrap to the desktop

1. If the Excel window is maximized, click the Restore button on its title bar.

2. Size Excel's window so the Windows desktop is visible.

3. Select a cell or range.

4. Click a border of the selection and drag it to the desktop.

After a scrap has served its purpose, you can right-click it and choose Delete to remove it from the desktop.

Editing a Cell's Contents

After you've entered information into a cell, it can be changed — or edited. When you want to edit the contents of a cell, you can use one of three ways to get into cell edit mode:

✦ Double-click the cell to edit the cell contents directly in the cell.

✦ Press F2. This lets you edit the cell contents directly in the cell.

✦ Activate the cell that you want to edit; then click in the formula bar to edit the cell contents in the formula bar.

All of these methods cause the formula bar to display three new mouse icons.

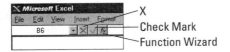

Icon	What It Does
X	Cancels editing, and the cell's contents aren't changed (Esc has the same effect)
Check Mark	Completes the editing and enters the modified contents into the cell (Enter has the same effect)
Function Wizard	Brings up Excel's Function Wizard, which makes it easy to enter a worksheet function into a formula

When you're editing the contents of a cell, the cursor changes to a vertical bar; you can move the vertical bar by using the direction keys. You can add new characters at the cursor location. Once you're in edit mode, you can use any of the following keys to perform your edits:

+ **Left/right arrow:** Moves the cursor left and right one character, respectively, without deleting any characters.

+ **Ctrl+left/right arrow:** Moves the cursor one group of characters to the left and right, respectively.

+ **Shift+left/right arrow:** Selects characters to the left or right of the cursor.

+ **Backspace:** Erases the character to the immediate left of the cursor.

+ **Delete:** Erases the character to the right of the cursor or erases all selected characters.

+ **Insert:** Places Excel in OVR (Overwrite) mode. Rather than add characters to the cell, you *overwrite*, or replace, existing characters with new ones, depending on the position of the cursor.

+ **Home:** Moves the cursor to the beginning of the cell entry.

+ **End:** Moves the cursor to the end of the cell entry.

+ **Enter:** Accepts the edited data.

Remember: If you change your mind after editing a cell, you can select Edit⇨Undo (or press Ctrl+Z) to restore the previous cell's contents. You must do this before entering any other data or using any other commands.

You also can use the mouse to select characters while you're editing a cell. Just click and drag the mouse pointer over the characters that you want to select.

Remember: If the cell is locked and the worksheet is protected, you can't make any changes to the cell unless you unprotect the worksheet (with the Tools⇨Protection⇨Unprotect Sheet command).

See also "Protecting a Worksheet," in Part II.

Entering Data into a Worksheet

Each worksheet in a workbook is made up of cells, and a cell can hold any of four types of data:

✦ A value (including a date or a time)

✦ Text

✦ A logical value (true or false)

✦ A formula, which returns a value, text, or a logical value

Remember: An Excel worksheet also can hold charts, drawings, diagrams, pictures, buttons, and other objects. These objects actually reside on the worksheet's *draw layer,* which is an invisible layer on top of each worksheet.

Entering data into a specific range

If you're entering data into a range of cells, you may want to select the entire range of cells before you start entering data. This causes Excel to move the cell pointer to the next cell in the selection when you press Enter.

Here's how it works:

✦ If the selection consists of multiple rows, Excel moves down the column; when it reaches the end of the column, it moves to the top of the next column.

✦ To skip a cell, just press Enter without entering anything.

✦ To go backward, use Shift+Enter. If you prefer to enter the data by rows rather than by columns, use Tab rather than Enter.

Entering dates and times

To Excel, a date or a time is simply a value — but it's formatted to appear as a date or a time.

Excel's system for working with dates uses a serial number system. The earliest date that Excel understands is January 1, 1900 (which has a serial number of 1). January 2, 1900, has a serial number of 2, and so on. This system makes it easy to deal with dates in formulas.

Normally, you don't have to be concerned with Excel's serial number date system. You can simply enter a date in a familiar format and Excel takes care of the details.

If you plan to use dates in formulas, make sure that the date you enter is actually recognized as a date; otherwise, your formulas will produce incorrect results. Excel is smart when it comes to recognizing dates that you enter into a cell, but it's not perfect. For example, Excel interprets the following entries as text, not dates:

✦ June 1 1995

✦ Jun-1 1995

✦ Jun-1/1995

Excel works with times by using fractional days. When working with times, you simply extend Excel's date serial number system to include decimals. For example, the date serial number for June 1, 1995, is 34851. Noon (halfway through the day) is represented internally as 34851.5.

The best way to deal with times is to enter the time into a cell in a recognized format. Here are some examples of time formats that Excel recognizes.

Entered into a Cell	Excel's Interpretation
11:30:00 am	11:30 a.m.
11:30:00 AM	11:30 a.m.
11:30 pm	11:30 p.m.
11:30	11:30 a.m.

You also can combine dates and times, however, as follows:

Entered into a Cell	Excel's Interpretation
6/1/95 11:30	11:30 a.m. on June 1, 1995

Entering formulas

A formula is a special type of cell entry that returns a result: When you enter a formula into a cell, the cell displays the result of the formula. The formula itself appears in the formula bar (which is just below the toolbars at the top of Excel's window) when the cell is activated.

A formula begins with an equal sign (=) and can consist of any of the following elements:

✦ Operators such as + (for addition) and * (for multiplication)

✦ Cell references, including addresses such as B4 or C12, as well as named cells and ranges

+ Values and text

+ Worksheet functions (such as SUM)

You can enter a formula into a cell in two ways: manually or by pointing to cell references.

To enter a formula manually

1. Move the cell pointer to the cell that will hold the formula.

2. Type an equal sign (=) to signal the fact that the cell contains a formula.

3. Enter the formula.

As you type, the characters appear in the cell as well as in the formula bar. You can use all of the normal editing keys (Delete, Backspace, direction keys, and so on) when entering a formula.

The pointing method of entering a formula still involves some manual typing, but you can simply point to the cell references rather than entering them manually, which is usually more accurate and less tedious.

To enter the formula **+A1/A2** into cell A3 by the pointing method

1. Move the cell pointer to cell A3.

2. Type an equal sign (=) to begin the formula.

3. Press the up arrow twice.

As you press this key, notice that Excel displays a faint moving border around the cell and that the cell reference appears in cell A3 and in the formula bar.

4. Type a division sign (/).

The faint border disappears and Enter reappears in the status bar at the bottom of the screen.

5. Press the up arrow one more time.

A2 is added to the formula.

6. Press Enter to end the formula.

Excel provides a set of toolbar tools that insert various characters into a formula for you. These tools aren't contained on any of the prebuilt toolbars, so you must create a custom toolbar to use them (or you can add them to an existing toolbar).

Entering fractions

To enter a fraction into a cell, leave a space between the whole number part and the fractional part. For example, to enter the decimal equivalent of 6 7/8

1. Enter **6**.

2. Enter a space.

3. Enter **7/8**.

4. Press Enter.

> Excel enters 6.875 into the cell and automatically formats the cell as a fraction.

If there is no whole number part (for example, 1/8), you must enter a zero and a space first, like this: **0 1/8**.

Entering text into cells

To enter text (rather than a value or a formula) into a cell

1. Move the cell pointer to the appropriate cell (this makes it the active cell).

2. Type the text (up to 255 characters).

3. Press Enter or any of the direction keys.

If you enter text that's longer than its column's current width, one of two things will happen.

✦ If the cells to the immediate right are blank, Excel displays the text in its entirety, spilling the entry into adjacent cells.

✦ If an adjacent cell is not blank, Excel displays as much of the text as possible. (The full text is contained in the cell; it's just not displayed.)

Remember: If you need to display a long text entry that's adjacent to a cell with an entry, you can edit your text to make it shorter, increase the width of the column, or wrap the text within the cell so that it occupies more than one line.

If you have lengthy text in a cell, you can force Excel to display it in multiple lines within the cell. Use Alt+Enter to start a new line in a cell. When you add this line break, Excel automatically changes the cell's format to Wrap Text.

See also "Wrapping text within a cell," in Part III.

Entering the current date or time into a cell

If you need to date-stamp or time-stamp your worksheet, Excel
provides two shortcut keys that do this for you:

+ **Current date:** Ctrl+; (semicolon)

+ **Current time:** Ctrl+Shift+; (semicolon)

Entering the same data into a range of cells

If you need to enter the same data (value, text, or a formula) into
multiple cells, your first inclination may be to enter it once and then
copy it to the remaining cells. Here's a better way:

1. Select all the cells that you want to contain the data.

2. Enter the value, text, or formula into one cell.

3. Press Ctrl+Enter.

   The single entry will be inserted into each cell in the selection.

Entering values into cells

To enter a numeric value into a cell

1. Move the cell pointer to the appropriate cell.

2. Enter the value.

3. Press Enter or any of the direction keys.

The value is displayed in the cell, and it also appears in Excel's
formula bar. You can also include a decimal point, dollar sign, plus
sign, minus sign, and comma. If you precede a value with a minus sign
or enclose it in parentheses, Excel considers the value to be a
negative number.

Remember: Sometimes the value won't be displayed exactly as you
enter it. Very large numbers may be converted to scientific notation.
For example, if you enter **123456789**, it will be displayed as **1.23E+08**.
This represents "1.23 times 10 to the eighth power." Notice, however,
that the formula bar displays the value that you entered originally.
Excel simply reformatted the value so that it would fit into the cell. If
you make the column wider, the number displays itself as you
entered it.

Erasing Data in Cells and Ranges

To erase the contents of a cell but leave the cell's formatting and notes intact

1. Select the cell or range you want to erase.

2. Press Delete.

For more control over what gets deleted, you can use the Edit⇨Clear command. This menu item leads to a submenu with four additional choices.

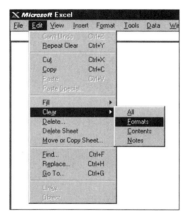

All	Clears everything from the cell
Formats	Clears only the formatting and leaves the value, text, or formula
Contents	Clears only the cell's contents and leaves the formatting
Notes	Clears the note (if one exists) attached to the cell

Moving Cells and Ranges

Moving the data in a cell or a range is common. For example, you may need to relocate a range of data to make room for something else.

Moving by dragging

To move a cell or range by dragging it

1. Select the cell or range to be moved.

2. Move the mouse pointer to one of the four borders of the selected cell or range.

When you do so, the mouse pointer turns into an arrow.

3. Drag the selection to its new location and release the mouse button.

This is similar to copying a cell, except that you don't press Ctrl while dragging.

Moving data to a different worksheet or workbook

If you want to move the contents of a cell or range to a different worksheet or to a different workbook

1. Select the cell or range to move.

 2. Select the Edit⇨Cut command. Or you can press Ctrl+X or click the Cut button on the Standard toolbar.

3. Activate the worksheet that you're moving to. If you're moving the selection to a different workbook, activate that workbook and then activate the worksheet.

4. Move the cell pointer to the range that will hold the copy (you need only select the upper-left cell).

5. Press Enter.

 When you move data, make sure that there are enough blank cells to hold it. Excel overwrites existing data without warning.

If the range that you're moving contains formulas that refer to other cells, the references to other cells will be invalid after moving the range.

Remember: If you change your mind after Step 2, press Esc to cancel the operation. If you change your mind after the data has already been copied, choose the Edit⇨Undo Paste command or press Ctrl+Z.

Moving data to a new location in the same worksheet

To move a cell or range

1. Select the cell or range to move.

2. Select the Edit⇨Cut command.

Or you can press Ctrl+X or click the Cut button on the Standard toolbar.

3. Move the cell pointer to the range that will hold the copy (you need only select the upper-left cell).

4. Press Enter.

If the range that you're moving contains formulas that refer to other cells, the references continue to refer to the original cells. You almost always want references to continue to refer to the original cells.

When you move data, make sure that there are enough blank cells to hold it. Excel overwrites existing data without warning.

Remember: If you change your mind after Step 2, press Esc to cancel the operation. If you change your mind after the data has already been copied, choose Edit⇨Undo Paste or press Ctrl+Z.

Replacing the Contents of a Cell

To replace the contents of a cell with something else

1. Select the cell.

2. Make your new entry (it replaces the previous contents).

Any formatting that you applied to the cell remains.

Searching for Data

If your worksheet contains lots of data, you may find it difficult to locate a particular piece of information. A quick way to do so is to let Excel do it for you.

To locate a particular value or sequence of text

1. Select the area of the worksheet that you want to search. If you want to search the entire worksheet, just select a single cell (any cell will do).

2. Choose the Edit⇨Find command or press Ctrl+F.

Excel displays its Find dialog box.

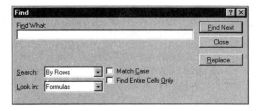

3. In the Fi_n_d What box, enter the characters to search for.

4. Specify what to look in: Formulas, Values, or Notes.

5. Click the Fi_n_d Next button.

Excel selects the cell that contains what you're looking for.

6. If there is more than one occurrence, repeat Step 5 until you find the cell that you're looking for.

7. Click the Close button to end.

For approximate searches, use *wildcard characters*. An asterisk represents any group of characters in the specified position, and a question mark represents any single character in the specified position. For example, **w*h** represents all text that begins with W and ends with H. Similarly, **b?n** matches three-letter words such as bin, bun, and ban.

See also "Searching and Replacing Data," in this part.

Searching and Replacing Data

Sometimes you may need to replace all occurrences of a value or text with something else. Excel makes this easy to do:

1. Select the area of the worksheet that you want to search. If you want to search the entire worksheet, just select a single cell (any cell will do).

2. Choose the E_d_it⇨Replace command or press Ctrl+H.

Excel displays the Replace dialog box.

3. In the Fi<u>n</u>d What box, enter the characters to search for.

4. In the R<u>e</u>place with box, enter the characters to replace them with.

5. Click the Replace <u>A</u>ll button to have Excel search and replace automatically.

If you would like to verify each replacement, click the <u>R</u>eplace button.

6. Click the Close button to end.

See also "Searching for Data," in this part.

Selecting Cells and Ranges

In Excel, you normally select a cell or range before performing an operation. Topics in this section describe how to make various types of cell and range selections.

Selecting a cell

To select a cell (and make it the active cell), use any of the following techniques:

✦ Move the cell pointer to the cell using the direction keys.

✦ Click the cell with the mouse.

✦ Use the <u>E</u>dit⇨<u>G</u>o To command (or press F5 or Ctrl+G), enter the cell address in the Reference box, and click OK.

The selected cell has a dark border around it, and its address appears in the Name box.

Selecting entire rows and columns

There are several ways to select entire rows or columns:

✦ Click the row or column border to select a single row or column.

✦ To select multiple adjacent rows or columns, simply click on a row or column border and drag to highlight additional rows or columns.

✦ To select multiple (nonadjacent) rows or columns, press Ctrl while you click on the rows or columns that you want.

✦ Press Ctrl+spacebar to select the column of the active cell.

✦ Press Shift+spacebar to select the row of the active cell.

✦ Click on the Select All button (or Ctrl+Shift+spacebar) to select all rows. Selecting all rows is the same as selecting all columns, which is the same as selecting all cells.

Selecting a multisheet (3-D) range

An Excel workbook can contain more than one worksheet, and a range can extend across multiple worksheets. You can think of these as three-dimensional ranges.

To select a multisheet range

1. Select the range on the active sheet.

2. Press Ctrl and click on the sheet tabs of the other sheets to include in the selection.

Notice that the title bar displays [Group]. This is a reminder that you've selected a group of sheets and that you're in Group Edit mode.

Once you've selected a multisheet range, you can perform the same operations that you can perform on a single sheet range.

If the multisheet range consists of a contiguous worksheet, you can press Shift and then click the tab of the last sheet to be included. Pressing Shift selects all sheets from the active sheet up to and including the sheet that you click.

Selecting noncontiguous ranges

Most of the time, the ranges that you select will be *contiguous* — a single rectangle of cells. Excel also lets you work with noncontiguous ranges, which consist of two or more ranges (or single cells), not necessarily next to each other (also known as a *multiple selection*).

If you want to apply the same formatting to cells in different areas of your worksheet, one approach is to make a multiple selection. When the appropriate cells or ranges are selected, the formatting that you select is applied to them all.

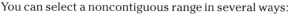
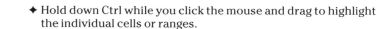

	A	B	C	D	E	F	G
4							
5	Sales Rep	Last Month	This Month	Change	Pct Change	Met Goal?	Com- mission
6	Murray	101,233	98,744	(2,489)	-2.5%	No	5,431
7	Knuckles	120,933	134,544	13,611	11.3%	No	7,400
8	Lefty	112,344	134,887	22,543	20.1%	Yes	8,768
9	Lucky	130,933	151,745	20,812	15.9%	Yes	9,863
10	Scarface	150,932	140,778	(10,154)	-6.7%	No	7,743
11	Totals	616,375	660,698	44,323	7.2%		39,205
12							
13	Average Rate:		5.93%				
14							
15							

You can select a noncontiguous range in several ways:

♦ Hold down Ctrl while you click the mouse and drag to highlight the individual cells or ranges.

♦ From the keyboard, select a range by pressing F8, then use the arrow keys. Then press Shift+F8 to select another range without canceling the previous range selections.

♦ Use the Edit⇨Go To command (or press F5 or Ctrl+G) and enter a range's address in the Reference box. Separate the different ranges with a comma. Click OK and Excel selects the cells in the ranges that you specified.

Selecting a range

You can select a range in several ways:

♦ Click the mouse in a cell and drag to highlight the range. If you drag to the end of the screen, the worksheet scrolls.

♦ Move to the first cell of the range. Press F8 and then move the cell pointer with the direction keys to highlight the range. Press F8 again to return the direction keys to normal movement.

♦ Another way to select a range using the keyboard is to press the Shift key while you use the direction keys to select a range.

♦ Use the Edit⇨Go To command (or press F5), enter a range's address in the Reference box, and click OK.

When you select a range, the cells appear in reverse video (the opposite color). The exception is the active cell, which remains its normal color though it now has a dark border.

Special selections

Excel provides a way to select only "special" cells in the workbook or in a selected range. These are cells that contain a certain type of information (see the table that follows).

1. Choose the Edit⇨Go To command, which brings up the Go To dialog box. You can also press F5 or Ctrl+G.

2. Click the Special button, displaying the Go To Special dialog box.

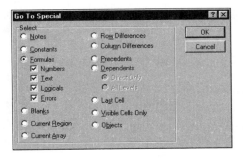

Following is a description of the options available in this dialog box.

Option	What It Does
Notes	Selects only the cells that contain cell notes (see "Using Cell Notes"). Ctrl + Shift + ? is the shortcut for this.
Constants	Selects all nonempty cells that don't contain formulas. This is useful if you have a model set up, and you want to clear out all input cells and enter new values. The formulas will remain intact.
Formulas	Selects cells that contain formulas. You can further qualify this by selecting the type of result: numbers, text, logical values (true or false), or errors.
Blanks	Selects all empty cells.
Current Region	Selects a rectangular range of cells around the active cell. This range is determined by surrounding blank rows and columns. Ctrl + * is the shortcut key for this.
Current Array	Selects the entire array. An array is a special type of formula used by advanced users.
Row Differences	Analyzes the selection and selects cells that are different from other cells in each row. Ctrl +\ is the shortcut for this.

continued

Option	What It Does
Column Differences	Analyzes the selection and selects the cells that are different from other cells in each column. Ctrl + Shift +	is the shortcut for this.
Precedents	Selects cells that are referred to in the formulas in the active cell or the selection. You can select either direct precedents or precedents at any level.
Dependents	Selects cells with formulas that refer to the active cell or the selection. You can select either direct dependents or dependents at any level.
Last Cell	Selects the bottom-right cell in the worksheet that contains data or formatting. Ctrl + End is the shortcut for this.
Visible Cells	Selects only visible cells in the selection. This is useful when dealing with outlines or an AutoFiltered list (see Part VI).
Objects	Selects all graphic objects on the worksheet.

After making your choice in the dialog box, Excel selects the qualifying subset of cells in the current selection. Usually, this results in a multiple selection (that is, a selection of noncontiguous cells).

Remember: If you bring up the Go To Special dialog box with only one cell selected, Excel bases its selection on the active area of the worksheet. If no cells qualify, Excel lets you know.

Transposing a range

If you need to change the orientation of a range, Excel can do it for you in a snap. When you transpose a range, rows become columns and columns become rows.

The following figure shows an example of a horizontal range that was transposed to a vertical range.

To transpose a range

1. Select the range to transpose.

2. Choose the Edit⇨Copy command, press Ctrl+C, or click the Copy button on the Standard toolbar.

3. Activate the upper-left cell where you want the transposed range to be. The transposed range cannot overlap with the original range.

4. Choose the Edit⇨Paste Special command.

5. Check the Transpose check box in the Paste Special dialog box.

6. Click OK.

7. Delete the original range, if necessary.

Remember: Any formulas in the original range are adjusted so that they work properly when transposed.

Undoing Changes and Mistakes

Excel has a single-level undo — which means that you can often recover from your errors. For example, if you accidentally delete a range of data, you can use the undo feature to retrieve the information.

To undo an operation, use any of the following:

✦ Select the Edit⇨Undo command. The command will tell you what you will be undoing.

✦ Press Ctrl+Z.

✦ Press Ctrl+Backspace.

If you make a mistake, it's important that you don't do anything else before you access the undo feature. Once you issue another command or make a cell entry, the operation that you wanted to undo can no longer be undone.

Using AutoFill

AutoFill is a handy feature that has several uses (mouse required). AutoFill uses the fill handle — the small square that appears at the bottom-right corner of the selected cell or range.

If you right-click and drag a fill handle, Excel displays a shortcut menu of fill options.

Book1

	A	B	C	D	E	F	G
1							
2	15-Sep	16-Sep					
3				Copy Cells			
4				Fill Series			
5				Fill Formats			
6				Fill Values			
7							
8				Fill Days			
9				Fill Weekdays			
10				Fill Months			
11				Fill Years			
12						.	
13				Linear Trend			
14				Growth Trend			
15				Series...			

Sheet1

Remember: If the selected cell or range does not have a fill handle, it means that this feature is turned off. To turn AutoFill back on

1. Select the Tools⇨Options command.

2. Click the Edit tab.

3. Check the check box labeled Allow Cell Drag and Drop.

For more on AutoFill, see Chapter 2 of *Excel For Windows 95 For Dummies,* by Greg Harvey, published by IDG Books Worldwide, Inc.

Entering a series of incremental values or dates

To use AutoFill to enter a series of incremental values

1. Enter at least two values or dates in the series into adjacent cells. These values need not be consecutive.

2. Select the cells you used in Step 1.

3. Click and drag the fill handle to complete the series in the cells that you select.

Remember: If you drag the fill handle when only one cell is selected, Excel simply copies the cell. However, if you drag the fill handle when a range of values is selected, Excel completes the series in the cells that you select.

AutoFill also works in the negative direction. For example, if you use AutoFill by starting with two cells that contain **-20** and **-19**, Excel fills in -18, -17, and so on.

If the values in the cells that you enter do not have equal increments, Excel completes the series by calculating a simple linear regression. This is handy for performing simple forecasts.

Entering a series of text

Excel is familiar with some text series (days of the week, month names), and you can have it complete these series for you automatically.

To use AutoFill to complete a known series of text

1. Enter any of the series into a cell (for example, **Monday** or **February**).

2. Click and drag the fill handle to complete the series in the cells that you select.

You can also teach Excel to recognize custom lists. Choose Tools⇨Options and click the Custom Lists tab. Click the NEW LIST option and enter your list. Your custom list also works with AutoFill.

Using Data Entry Forms

If you're entering data that is arranged in rows, you may find it helpful to use Excel's built-in data form for data entry.

Using Excel's built-in data form

To enter data using a data entry form

1. If your data entry ranges do not have descriptive headings in the first row, enter them. You can always erase these headings later if you don't need them.

2. Select any cell in the header row.

3. Choose the Data⇨Form command.

Excel asks whether you want to use that row for headers (answer Yes). It then displays a dialog box with edit boxes and several buttons.

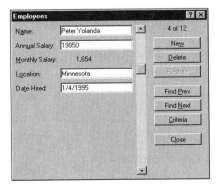

Use Tab to move between the edit boxes. When you complete entering the data for a row, click the Ne<u>w</u> button. Excel dumps the data into the worksheet and clears the dialog box for the next row.

See also "Filtering and Sorting Lists," in Part VI.

Using AutoComplete

AutoComplete, new to Excel 95, lets you type the first few letters of a text entry into a cell, and Excel automatically completes the entry based on other entries that you've already made in the column.

AutoComplete works with no effort on your part:

1. Begin entering text or a value.

2. If Excel recognizes your entry, it automatically completes it.

3. If Excel guesses correctly, press Enter to accept it. If you want to enter something else, just continue typing and ignore Excel's guess.

You also can access this feature by right-clicking on the cell and selecting Pick from list. With this method, Excel displays a drop-down box with all of the entries in the current column. Just click the one that you want, and it's entered automatically.

If you don't like this feature, you can turn it off in the Edit panel of the Options dialog box. Remove the check mark from the check box labeled Enable Auto<u>C</u>omplete for Cell Values.

Using Automatic Decimal Points

If you're entering lots of numbers with a fixed number of decimal places, you may be interested in this tip that lets you omit the decimal points (like the feature available on some adding machines).

1. Select the <u>T</u>ools⇨<u>O</u>ptions command.

2. Click the Edit tab.

3. Check the check box labeled Fi<u>x</u>ed Decimal and make sure that it's set for the number of decimal places that you'll be using.

This causes Excel to supply the decimal points for you automatically. For example, if you have it set for two decimal places and you enter **12345** into a cell, Excel interprets it as 123.45 (it adds the decimal point). To restore things to normal, just uncheck the Fixed Decimal check box in the Options dialog box.

Remember: Changing this setting doesn't affect any values that you have already entered.

Using Cell Notes

Excel's cell note feature lets you attach a note to a cell — useful when you need to document a particular value or to help you remember what a formula does. When you move the mouse pointer over a cell that has a note, the note pops up in a small box.

Adding a cell note

To add a note to a cell

1. Select the cell.

2. Choose the Insert⇨Note command (or press Shift+F2).

Excel displays the Cell Note dialog box.

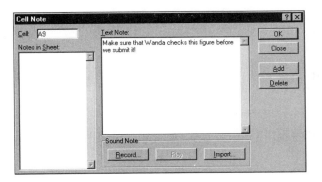

3. Enter the text for the note into the Text Note box and click OK.

You can add notes to multiple cells without closing the dialog box. Use the Add button to add a note and then select the next cell using the Cell edit box. When you're finished adding cell notes, click OK.

Using sound notes

If your computer is equipped with a sound card and microphone, you also can add an audio (sound) note to the cell (or import a sound file). You might use this feature to record some comments into a workbook that you are giving to someone else.

1. Select the cell.

2. Choose the Insert⇨Note command (or press Shift+F2).

Excel displays the Cell Note dialog box.

3. Click on the Record button to record an audio note or click the Import button to import a sound file, which must be in the WAV format.

To play a sound note, just move the mouse pointer over the cell.

Be careful with sound notes because they take up lots of memory and storage space. Using audio notes can make the size of your workbook increase significantly.

Viewing cell notes

Cells that have a note attached display a small red dot in the upper-right corner. When you move the mouse pointer over a cell that contains a note, Excel displays the note in a pop-up box (similar to the tooltips for toolbar buttons).

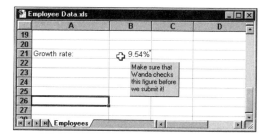

This is a new feature in Excel 95. In former versions, the only way to view a cell note was to use the Insert⇔Note command.

Part V

Using Formulas and Functions

This part deals with topics related to formulas and functions. It also covers related topics that deal with data consolidation and auditing.

In this part . . .

- ✔ Consolidating data in multiple worksheets
- ✔ Entering formulas
- ✔ Working with formulas that contain links
- ✔ Creating and using range names
- ✔ Using Excel's built-in worksheet functions
- ✔ Identifying worksheet errors

Consolidating Data

Data consolidation refers to the process of merging data from multiple worksheets or multiple workbook files. For example, a division manager may consolidate departmental budgets into a single workbook.

The main factor that determines how easy a consolidation task will be is whether the information is laid out exactly the same way in each worksheet. If so, the job is relatively simple.

If the worksheets have little or no resemblance to each other, your best bet may be to edit each sheet so that they match each other. In some cases, it may be more efficient to simply reenter the information in a standard format.

Any of the following techniques will consolidate information from multiple worksheets or workbooks:

✦ Use formulas (link formulas if the data is in multiple workbooks).

✦ Use Excel's Data⇨Consolidate command.

✦ Use a pivot table.

See also "Pivot Tables," in Part VI.

Consolidating data by matching labels

If the worksheets to be consolidated are not laid out identically, you may still be able to use Excel's Data⇨Consolidate command. The worksheets must have identical row and column labels, because Excel uses this information to match the data.

1. Start with a new workbook. The source workbooks can be open, but this is not necessary.

2. Select the Data⇨Consolidate command to open the Consolidate dialog box.

3. Select the type of consolidation summary that you want. Most of the time you'll use Sum.

4. Enter the range reference for the first worksheet.

If the workbook is open, you can point to the reference. If it's not open, click the Browse button to locate the file on disk. The reference must include a range. When the reference in the Reference box is correct, click Add to add it to the All References list.

5. Repeat Step 4 for each additional worksheet.

6. Because the worksheets aren't laid out the same, select the Left Column and Top Row check boxes to match the data by using the labels in the worksheet.

7. Click OK to begin the consolidation.

See also "Using the Consolidate dialog box," in this part, for an explanation of the various options in the Consolidate dialog box.

Consolidating data by position

If the worksheets to be consolidated are laid out identically, you can use Excel's Data⇨Consolidate command:

1. Start with a new workbook.

The source workbooks can be open, but this is not necessary.

2. Select the Data⇨Consolidate command to display the Consolidate dialog box.

3. Select the type of consolidation summary that you want.

Most of the time you'll use Sum.

4. Enter the range reference for the first worksheet.

If the workbook is open, you can point to the reference. If it's not open, click the Browse button to locate the file on disk. The reference must include a range. When the reference in the Reference box is correct, click Add to add it to the All References list.

5. Repeat Step 4 for each additional worksheet.

6. Click OK to begin the consolidation.

Excel creates the consolidation beginning at the active cell.

See also "Using the Consolidate dialog box," in this part, for an explanation of the various options in the Consolidate dialog box.

Consolidating data by using formulas

You can consolidate information across worksheets by creating formulas that refer to cells in the source worksheets. To consolidate data by using formulas

1. Start with an empty worksheet.

2. Create a formula that adds the cells in each of the source worksheets.

3. If the source worksheets are laid out identically, copy the formula created in Step 2.

If the source worksheets have different layouts, you need to create each formula separately.

Remember: Using formulas in this manner ensures that the consolidation formulas will be updated if the source data changes.

See also "Referencing cells in other workbooks" and "Referencing cells in other worksheets," both in this part.

Using the Consolidate dialog box

Following is a description of the options in Consolidate dialog box.

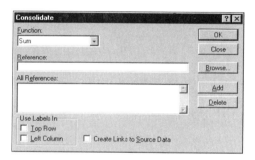

Function: This is where you specify the type of consolidation. Most of the time you'll use Sum, but you also can select from ten other options.

Reference: This holds a range from a source file that will be consolidated. After the range is entered, click the Add button to add it to the All References list. If you're consolidating by position, don't include labels in the range. If you're consolidating by matching labels, *do* include labels in the range.

All References: This list box contains the list of references that you have added with the Add button.

Use Labels In: These check boxes tell Excel to examine the labels in the top row, the left column, or both positions to perform the consolidation. Use these options when you're consolidating by category.

Create Links to Source Data: This option, when selected, creates an outline in the destination worksheet that consists of external references to the destination cells (that is, link formulas). In addition, the outline includes summary formulas. If this option isn't selected, the consolidation won't use formulas.

Browse: This button displays a dialog box that lets you select a workbook on disk. It inserts the filename in the Reference box, but you have to supply the range reference.

Add: This button adds the reference in the Reference box to the All References list.

Delete: This button deletes the selected reference from the All Reference list.

See also "Consolidating data by position" and "Consolidating data by matching labels," both in this part.

Using Formulas

A formula can consist of up to 1,024 characters and any of the following elements:

✦ Operators such as + (for addition) and * (for multiplication)

✦ Cell references (including named cells and ranges)

✦ Values, text, or logical values

✦ Worksheet functions (such as Sum)

When you enter a formula into a cell, the cell displays the result of the formula. You see the formula itself in the formula bar when the cell is activated.

Following is a list of operators that you can use in formulas.

Operator	Name
+	Addition
-	Subtraction
*	Multiplication
/	Division
^	Exponentiation (raised to a power)
&	Concatenation (joins text)
=	Logical comparison (equal to)
>	Logical comparison (greater than)
<	Logical comparison (less than)

Operator precedence is the set of rules that Excel uses to perform its calculations in a formula. The table below lists Excel's operator precedence. This table shows that exponentiation has the highest precedence (that is, it's performed first), and logical comparisons have the lowest precedence.

Symbol	Operator	Precedence
^	Exponentiation	1
*	Multiplication	2
/	Division	2
+	Addition	3
-	Subtraction	3
&	Concatenation	4
=	Equal to	5
<	Less than	5
>	Greater than	5

Remember: You can override operator precedence by using parentheses in your formulas.

For more on using formulas, see Chapter 2 and other sections of *Excel For Windows 95 For Dummies*.

Changing the source of links

If your workbook uses one or more formulas that contain links to other workbooks, you may need to change the source workbook for your external references. For example, you may have a worksheet that has links to a workbook named Preliminary Budget. Later, you get a finalized version named Final Budget.

To change the link source

1. Select the Edit⇨Links command.

2. In the Links dialog box, select the source workbook that you want to change.

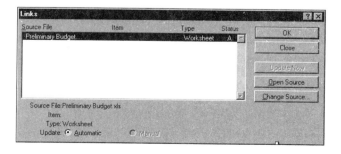

3. Click the Change Source button.

4. In the Change Links dialog box, select a new source file.

After you select the file, all external reference formulas are updated.

Changing when formulas are calculated

When Excel's Calculation mode is set to Automatic (the default setting), changing cells that are used in a formula causes the formula to display a new result automatically. Excel follows these rules when calculating your worksheet:

✦ When you make a change (enter or edit data or formulas, for example), Excel immediately re-calculates those formulas that depend on new or edited data.

✦ If Excel is in the middle of a lengthy calculation, the calculation is temporarily suspended while you perform other worksheet tasks; it resumes when you're finished.

✦ Formulas are evaluated in a natural sequence. In other words, if a formula in cell D12 depends on the result of a formula in cell D11, cell D11 is calculated before D12.

To set Excel's Calculation mode to Manual

1. Choose the Tools⇨Options command.

2. Click the Calculation tab.

3. Click the Manual option button.

When you switch to Manual Calculation mode, the Recalculate Before Save check box is automatically turned on. You can turn this off if you want to speed up file-save operations.

Remember: When you're working in Manual Calculation mode, Excel displays Calculate in the status bar when you have any uncalculated formulas. Use the following shortcut keys to recalculate the formulas:

✦ F9: Calculates the formulas in all open workbooks.

✦ Shift+F9: Calculates only the formulas in the active worksheet. Other worksheets in the same workbook won't be calculated.

Remember: Excel's Calculation mode isn't specific to a particular worksheet. When you change Excel's Calculation mode, all open workbooks are affected, not just the active workbook.

Calculating subtotals

Excel's ability to create subtotal formulas automatically is a handy feature that can save you lots of time. To use this feature, you must have a list that is sorted.

To insert subtotal formulas into a list

1. Move the cell pointer anywhere in the list.

2. Choose the Data⇨Subtotals command.

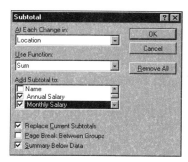

3. Complete the Subtotal dialog box by specifying the options described below. The formulas all use the Subtotal worksheet function to insert the subtotals.

Following is a list of Options available for subtotals:

At Each Change in	This drop-down list displays the columns in your list. The column that you choose must be sorted.
Use Function	This gives you a choice of 11 functions. Usually, you'll want to use Sum (the default).
A**d**d Subtotal to	This list box lists all of the fields in your list. Place a check mark next to the field or fields that you want to subtotal.
Replace **C**urrent Subtotals	If this box is checked, any existing subtotal formulas are removed and replaced with the new subtotals.
Page Break Between Groups	If this box is checked, Excel inserts a manual page break after each subtotal.
Summary Below Data	If this box is checked, the subtotals are placed below the data (the default). Otherwise, the subtotal formulas are placed above the totals.
Remove All	This button removes all of the subtotal formulas in the list.

4. Click OK and Excel analyzes the list and inserts formulas as specified — and also creates an outline for you.

Converting formulas to values

Sometimes, you may want to convert a formula to its current value (remove the formula and leave only its result). To do so

1. Select the cell that contains the formula. If you want to convert several formulas you can select a range.

2. Choose the Edit⇨Copy command (you can also press Ctrl+C or click the Copy button on the Standard toolbar).

3. Choose the Edit⇨Paste Special command.

4. In the Paste Special dialog box, select the Values option button.

5. Click OK.

6. Press Enter to cancel Copy mode.

Remember: The procedure above overwrites the formulas. If you want to put the current values of the formulas in a different (empty) area of the worksheet, select a different range before Step 3 in the preceding list.

Identifying formula errors

Excel flags errors in formulas with a message that begins with a pound sign (#). This signals that the formula is returning an error value. You'll have to correct the formula (or correct a cell that is referenced by the formula) to get rid of the error display.

Remember: If the entire cell is filled with pound signs, this means that the column isn't wide enough to display the value.

The following table lists the types of error values that may appear in a cell that has a formula.

Error Value	Explanation
#DIV/0!	The formula is trying to divide by zero (an operation that's not allowed on this planet). This also occurs when the formula attempts to divide by an empty cell.
#NAME?	The formula uses a name that Excel doesn't recognize. This can happen if you delete a name that's used in the formula or if you have unmatched quotes when using text.
#N/A	The formula is referring (directly or indirectly) to a cell that uses the NA functions to signal the fact that data is not available.
#NULL!	The formula uses an intersection of two ranges that don't intersect.
#NUM!	There is a problem with a value; for example, you specified a negative number where a positive number is expected.
#REF!	The formula refers to a cell that isn't valid. This can happen if the cell has been deleted from the worksheet.
#VALUE!	The formula has a function with an invalid argument, or the formula uses an operand of the wrong type (such as text where a value is expected).

Remember: A single error value can make its way to lots of other cells that contain formulas that depend on the cell.

Pasting names into a formula

If your formula uses named cells or ranges, you can type the name in place of the address. A less error-prone approach is to choose the name from a list and have Excel insert the name for you automatically. There are three ways to do this:

✦ Select the Insert⇨Name⇨Paste command. Excel displays its Paste Name dialog box with all of the names listed. Select the name and click OK.

✦ Press F3. This also displays the Paste Name dialog box.

✦ Click on the Name box and select a name from the list.

Remember: The Name box displays only the first 100 names in the workbook, in alphabetical order.

See also topics in "Using Names," in this part.

Referencing cells in other workbooks

If your formula needs to refer to a cell in a different workbook, use this format for your formula:

```
=[WorkbookName]SheetName!CellAddress
```

The cell address is preceded by the workbook name (in brackets), the worksheet name, and an exclamation point. Such a formula is sometimes known as a *link formula*.

Remember: If the workbook name in the reference includes one or more spaces, you must enclose it (and the sheet name) in single quotation marks. For example, here's a formula that refers to a cell on Sheet1 in a workbook named Budget For 1996:

```
+A1*'[Budget For 1996]Sheet1'!A1
```

When a formula refers to cells in a different workbook, the other workbook doesn't need to be open. If the workbook is closed, you must add the complete path to the reference. Here's an example:

```
+A1*'C:\MSOffice\Excel\[Budget For 1996]Sheet1'!A1
```

Referencing cells in other worksheets

If your formula needs to refer to a cell in a different worksheet in the same workbook, use the following format for your formula:

```
SheetName!CellAddress
```

Precede the cell address with the worksheet name, followed by an exclamation point.

Remember: If the worksheet name in the reference includes one or more spaces, you must enclose it in single quotation marks. Here's a formula that refers to a cell on a sheet named All Depts:

```
+A1*'All Depts'!A1
```

Severing (cutting) links

If you have external references in a workbook (that is, a link to a different workbook) and then decide that you don't want them, you can convert the external reference formulas to values, thereby severing the links:

1. Select the cell or range that contains the external reference formulas.

 2. Click the Copy button on the Standard toolbar to copy the selection to the Clipboard.

3. Choose the Edit⇨Paste Special command.

4. In the Paste Special dialog box, select the Values option.

5. Click OK.

6. Press Esc to cancel Copy mode.

All formulas in the selected range are converted to their current values.

Updating links

To ensure that your link formulas have the latest values from their source workbooks, you can force an update. This may be necessary if you just learned that someone made changes to the source workbook and saved the latest version on your network server.

To update linked formulas with their current value

1. Select the Edit⇨Links command.

2. In the Links dialog box, choose the appropriate source workbook.

3. Click the Update Now button.

Excel updates the link formulas.

Using absolute and mixed references

An *absolute reference* uses two dollar signs in its address: one for the column part and one for the row part. When you copy a formula that has an absolute reference, the reference is not adjusted in the copied cell. *Relative references*, on the other hand, are adjusted when the formula is copied.

Excel also allows mixed references in which only one of the address's parts is absolute. The following table summarizes all of the possible types of cell references.

Example	Type
A1	Relative reference
A1	Absolute reference
$A1	Mixed reference (column part is absolute)
A$1	Mixed reference (row part is absolute)

To change the type of cell reference in a formula

1. Double-click the cell (or press F2) to get into edit mode.

2. In the formula bar, move the cursor to a cell reference.

3. Press F4 repeatedly to cycle through all possible cell reference types. Stop when the cell reference displays the proper type.

Using Functions in Your Formulas

Excel provides more than 300 built-in functions that can make your formulas perform powerful feats and save you a great deal of time.

Functions

✦ Simplify your formulas.

✦ Allow formulas to perform calculations that are otherwise impossible.

✦ Speed up some editing tasks.

✦ Allow "conditional" execution of formulas — giving them some rudimentary decision-making capability.

You can use Excel's VBA language to create your own custom functions if you're so inclined.

Most, but not all, worksheet functions use one or more arguments, enclosed in parentheses. Think of an argument as a piece of information that clarifies what you want the function to do. For example, the function below (which rounds the number in cell A1 to two decimal places) uses two arguments:

=ROUND(A1,2)

Entering functions manually

If you're familiar with the function that you want to use, you may choose to simply type the function and its arguments into your formula. Often this is the most efficient method.

Remember: If you're using a function at the beginning of a formula, you must provide an initial equal sign (=).

When you enter a function, Excel always converts it to uppercase. It's a good idea to use lowercase when entering functions: If Excel doesn't convert it to uppercase, it means that it doesn't recognize your entry as a function (you probably spelled it incorrectly).

Using add-in functions

Some functions are available only when a particular add-in is open. To use add-in worksheet functions

1. Select the Tools➪Add-Ins command.

2. Check the box next to the add-in that contains the functions you need.

3. Click OK.

You can then use the add-in functions in your formulas.

Remember: If you attempt to use an add-in function when the add-in is not loaded, the formula will display #NAME?

Using the Function Wizard

Excel's *Function Wizard* makes it easy to enter a function and its arguments. Using the Function Wizard ensures that the function is spelled correctly and has the proper number of arguments in the correct order.

Any of these options displays the first of two Function Wizard dialog boxes.

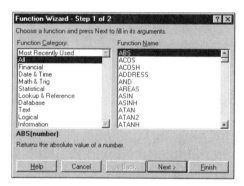

1. Activate the cell that will contain the function.

2. Invoke the Function Wizard, using any of the following techniques.

   • Choose the Insert⇨Function command from the menu.

    • Click the Function Wizard button on the Standard toolbar.

   • Press Shift+F3.

   • Click the Function Wizard icon on the formula bar (available only when you're entering or editing a formula).

3. Choose 1 from the 11 function categories in the Function Category list box (there may be more function categories if custom functions are available).

4. Locate the function you want in the Function Name list box.

   The dialog box shows the function and its list of arguments and also displays a brief description of the function.

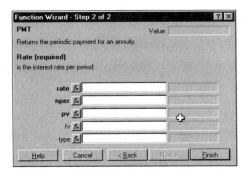

5. Click the Next button.

Excel displays the second Function Wizard dialog box, which prompts you for the function's arguments.

6. Enter the arguments into the appropriate edit boxes.

You can enter the arguments manually, or (if they are cell references) point to them in the worksheet.

7. When you've specified all of the required arguments, click the Finish button.

Remember: You can use the Function Wizard to insert a function into an existing formula. Just edit the formula and move the cursor to the location where you want to insert the function. Then invoke the Function Wizard and make your choices.

If the active cell is not empty when you invoke the Function Wizard, the contents are overwritten.

Using Names

Excel lets you provide names for cells and ranges. Using names offers the following advantages:

✦ A meaningful range name (such as Total_Income) is much easier to remember than a cell address (such as AC21).

✦ You can quickly move to areas of your worksheet by using the Name box, located at the left side of the formula bar (click on the arrow to drop down a list of defined names) or by choosing the Edit⇨Go To command (or F5) and specifying the range name.

✦ When you select a named cell or range, the name appears in the Name box.

✦ Creating formulas is easier. You can paste a cell or range name into a formula by using the Insert➪Name➪Paste command or by selecting a name from the Name box.

✦ Names make your formulas more understandable and easier to use. =Income-Taxes is more intuitive than =D20-D40.

✦ Macros are easier to create and maintain when you use range names rather than cell addresses.

Although Excel is quite flexible about the names that you can define, it does have some rules:

✦ Names can't contain any spaces. You may want to use an underscore or a period character to simulate a space (such as Annual_Total or Annual.Total).

✦ You can use any combination of letters and numbers, but the name must not begin with a number (such as 3rdQuarter) or look like a cell reference (such as Q3).

✦ Most symbols aren't allowed. However, you can use underscore (_), period (.), backslash (\), and question mark (?).

✦ Names are limited to 255 characters.

✦ You can use single letters (except for R or C), but I don't recommend this because it defeats the purpose of using meaningful names.

Excel also uses a few names internally for its own use. Avoid using the following for names: Print_Area, Print_Titles, Consolidate_Area, and Sheet_Title.

Applying names to existing cell references

When you create a new name for a cell or a range, Excel doesn't automatically use the name in place of existing references in your formulas. For example, if you have a formula such as +A1*20 and then give a name to cell A1, the formula will continue to display A1 (not the new name). However, it's fairly easy to replace cell or range references with their corresponding names.

To apply names to cell references in existing formulas

1. Select the range that you want to modify.

2. Choose the Insert➪Name➪Apply command.

3. In the Apply Names dialog box, select the names that you want to apply by clicking them.

4. Click OK. Excel replaces the range references with the names in the selected cells.

Changing names

Excel doesn't have a simple way to change a name after it's created. If you create a name and then realize that it's not the name you wanted (or, perhaps, that you spelled it incorrectly)

1. Create the new name, using any of the techniques described in this part.

2. Delete the old name.

See also "Deleting names," in this part.

See also "Creating names automatically," "Creating names with the Define Name dialog box," and "Creating names using the Name box," all in this part.

Creating a table of names

You may want to create a list of all names in the workbook. This may be useful for tracking down errors or as a way to document your work.

To create a table of names

1. Move the cell pointer to an empty area of your worksheet (the table will be created at the active cell position).

2. Choose the Insert⇨Name⇨Paste command (or press F3).

3. Click the Paste List button in the Paste Name dialog box.

The list that Excel pastes overwrites any cells that get in the way, so make sure that the active cell is located in an empty portion of the worksheet.

Creating names automatically

Your worksheet may contain text that you want to use for names for adjacent cells or ranges. For example, you may have month names in column A and corresponding sales figures in column B. You can create a name for each cell in column B by using the text in column A.

To create names using adjacent text

1. Select the name text and the cells that you want to name (these can be individual cells or ranges of cells).

The names must be adjacent to the cells you're naming (a multiple selection is not allowed here).

2. Choose the Insert⇨Name⇨Create command (or Ctrl+Shift+F3).

Excel will guess how to create the names.

3. Adjust the check boxes in the Create Names dialog box (if necessary) to correspond to the manner in which you want to create the names.

4. Click OK to create the names.

Remember: If the text contained in a cell results in an invalid name, Excel modifies the name to make it valid. If Excel encounters a value or a formula where text should be, however, it doesn't convert it to a valid name. It simply doesn't create a name.

Creating names using the Name box

To create a name using the Name box

1. Select the cell or range to name.

2. Click the Name box and enter the name.

3. Press Enter to create the name.

Remember: If a name already exists, you can't use the Name box to change the reference that the name refers to. Attempting to do so will simply select the name that you enter.

Creating names with the Define Name dialog box

To create a range name using the Define Name dialog box

1. Select the cell or range that you want to name.

2. Choose the Insert⇨Name⇨Define command (or press Ctrl+F3).

Excel displays the Define Name dialog box.

3. Type a name in the edit box labeled Names in Workbook (or use the name that Excel proposes, if any).

The active or selected cell or range address appears in the Refers to text box.

4. Verify that the address listed is correct and then click OK to add the name to your worksheet.

5. Click OK to close the dialog box.

Or you can click the Add button to continue adding names to your worksheet. If you do this, you must specify the Refers to range by typing an address (make sure to begin with an equal sign) or by pointing to it in the worksheet. Each name appears in the list box.

Deleting names

If you no longer need a defined name, you can delete it:

1. Choose the Insert⇨Name⇨Define command.

2. In the Define Name dialog box, select the name that you want to delete from the list.

3. Click the Delete button.

Be extra careful when deleting names. If the name is used in a formula, deleting the name causes the formula to become invalid (it will display #NAME?). Even worse, deleting a name can't be undone. It's a good practice to save your workbook before you delete any names.

Remember: If you delete the rows or columns that contain named cells or ranges, the names contain an invalid reference. For example, if cell A1 on Sheet1 is named Interest and you delete row 1 or column A, Interest then refers to =Sheet1!#REF! (that is, an erroneous reference). If you use Interest in a formula, the formula will display #REF.

Redefining names

After you've defined a name, you may want to change the cell or range to which it refers:

1. Select the Insert⇨Name⇨Define command.

2. In the Define Name dialog box, select the name that you want to change.

3. Edit the cell or range address in the Refers to edit box.

If you like, you can click the edit box and select a new cell or range by pointing in the worksheet.

Using multisheet names

Names can extend into the third dimension — across multiple worksheets in a workbook. To create a multisheet name

1. Choose the Insert⇨Name⇨Define command.

2. Enter the name in the Names in Workbook box in the Define Name dialog box.

3. Enter the reference in the Refers to box manually. The format for a multisheet reference is as follows:

```
FirstSheet:LastSheet!RangeReference
```

Remember: This name won't appear in the Name box, however, or in the Go To dialog box. Excel lets you define the name but it doesn't give you a way to automatically select the cells to which the name refers.

Using sheet level names

Normally, a name that you create can be used anywhere within the workbook. Names, by default, are "book level" names rather than "sheet level" names. But what if you have several worksheets in a workbook and you want to use the same name (such as Dept_Total) on each sheet? That's when you need to create sheet level names.

To define a sheet level name

1. Activate the worksheet where you want to define the name.

2. Choose the Insert⇨Name⇨Define command.

3. In the Names in Workbook box, enter the name, but precede it with the worksheet name and an exclamation point. For example, **Sheet2!Dept_Total.**

4. In the Refers to box, enter the cell or range the name refers to.

You also can create a sheet level name by using the Name box. Select the cell or range, activate the Name box, and enter the name, preceded by the sheet's name and an exclamation point.

Remember: When you write a formula that uses a sheet level name on the sheet where it's defined, you don't need to include the worksheet name in the range name (the Name box won't display the worksheet name either). If you use the name in a formula on a different worksheet, however, you must use the entire name (sheet name, exclamation point, and name).

Workbook Auditing

Auditing refers to the process of tracking down and identifying errors in your workbook.

Handling circular references

When you're entering formulas, you may occasionally see a message from Excel like the one shown below. This indicates that the formula you just entered will result in a circular reference.

A *circular reference* occurs when a formula refers to its own value (either directly or indirectly).

When you get the circular reference message after entering a formula, Excel lets you enter the formula and displays a message in the status bar to remind you that a circular reference exists. Most of the time, a circular reference indicates an error that must be corrected.

Remember: Excel won't tell you about a circular reference if the Iteration setting is on. You can check this in the Options dialog box (in the Calculation panel). If Iteration is on, Excel performs the circular calculation the number of times specified in the Maximum Iterations field (or until the value changes by less than .001 — or whatever value is in the Maximum Change field).

There are a few situations (known about by advanced users) in which you would use a circular reference intentionally. In these cases, the Iteration setting must be on. It's best, however, to keep the Iteration setting off so that you'll be warned of circular references.

Using Excel's auditing tools

Excel provides a set of interactive auditing tools that you may find helpful. These tools can be accessed by using the Tools⇨Auditing command (which results in a submenu with additional choices) or from the Auditing toolbar.

The tools on the Auditing toolbar are as follows:

 ◆ **Trace Precedents:** Draws arrows to indicate a formula cell's precedents. You can click this multiple times to see additional levels of precedents.

 ◆ **Remove Precedent Arrows:** Removes the most recently placed set of precedent arrows.

 ◆ **Trace Dependents:** Draws arrows to indicate a cell's dependents. You can click this multiple times to see additional levels of dependents.

 ◆ **Remove Dependent Arrows:** Removes the most recently placed set of dependent arrows.

 ◆ **Remove All Arrows:** Removes all precedent and dependent arrows from the worksheet.

 ◆ **Trace Error:** Draws arrows from a cell that contains an error to the cells that may have caused the error.

 ◆ **Attach Note:** Displays the Cell Note dialog box. This doesn't have much to do with auditing. It just lets you attach a note to a cell.

 ◆ **Show Info Window:** Displays the Info Window (described later).

These tools can identify precedents and dependents by drawing arrows (known as cell tracers) on the worksheet.

Remember: Precedents are cells that are referred to by a formula (either directly or indirectly). Dependents are formulas that depend on a particular cell.

Excel also has some shortcut keys that you can use to select precedents and dependents. These are

Key Combination	What It Selects
Ctrl+[	Direct precedents
Ctrl+Shift+[	All precedents
Ctrl+]	Direct dependents
Ctrl+Shift+]	All dependents

Using the Info window

Excel has a very useful feature called the *Info window,* a free-floating window that displays useful information about the active cell. It's read-only, so you can't make any changes to the information.

To display the Info window

1. Choose the Tools➪Options command.

2. Click the View tab in the Options dialog box.

3. Check the box labeled Info Window.

To close the Info window, click the Close button in its title bar.

By default, the Info window shows only the cell address, the formula, and the cell note. You can determine what type of information is shown in the Info window. When the window is active, a new menu (Info) is available. Use this menu to select the type of information to display.

Remember: The options that you select for the Info window aren't saved; you need to reselect them every time you open the Info window.

Viewing formulas

One way to audit your workbook is to display the formulas rather than the results of the formulas. Then you can examine the formulas without having to scroll through the worksheet. To do this

1. Select the Tools⇨Options command.

2. Click the View tab of the Options dialog box.

3. Check the box labeled Formulas.

You may want to create a new window for the workbook before issuing this command. That way, you can see the formulas in one window and the results in the other.

Part VI

Analyzing Spreadsheet Data

Much of what you do with Excel involves analyzing data. This part deals with a variety of topics related to data analysis.

In this part . . .

- ✔ Managing lists of data maintained in a worksheet
- ✔ Sorting and filtering lists
- ✔ Accessing data stored in external database files
- ✔ Performing what-if analysis
- ✔ Creating data tables
- ✔ Using Excel's scenario management tools
- ✔ Using pivot tables
- ✔ Using goal seeking
- ✔ Using the Analysis ToolPak add-in

Filtering and Sorting Lists

Information of just about any type can be stored in a list. If you're familiar with the concept of a database table, you'll recognize that a list has many similarities:

✦ Columns correspond to fields.

✦ Rows correspond to records.

✦ The first row of the table should have field names that describe the data in each column.

Use the <u>W</u>indow⇨<u>F</u>reeze Panes command to make sure that the headings are always visible when the list is scrolled.

See also "Freezing row or column titles," in Part II.

You can preformat entire columns to ensure that the data will have the same format. For example, if a column contains dates, format the entire column with the desired date format.

Remember: The size of the lists that you develop in Excel is limited by the size of a single worksheet. Therefore, a list can have no more than 256 fields and can consist of no more than 16,383 records (one row contains the field names).

See also "Using data entry forms," in Part IV.

Applying database functions with lists

To create a formula that returns results based on filtered criteria, use Excel's database worksheet functions. For example, you can create a formula that calculates the sum of values in a list that meet a certain criteria. Set up a criteria range and then enter a formula such as the following:

```
=DSUM(ListRange,FieldName,Criteria)
```

In this case, *ListRange* refers to the list, *FieldName* refers to the field name cell of the column that is being summed, and *Criteria* refers to the criteria range.

Excel's database functions are listed as follows.

Function	Description
DAVERAGE	Returns the average of selected database entries
DCOUNT	Counts the cells containing numbers from a specified database and criteria

Function	Description
DCOUNTA	Counts nonblank cells from a specified database and criteria
DGET	Extracts from a database a single record that matches the specified criteria
DMAX	Returns the maximum value from selected database entries
DMIN	Returns the minimum value from selected database entries
DPRODUCT	Multiplies the values in a particular field of records that match the criteria in a database
DSTDEV	Estimates the standard deviation based on a sample of selected database entries
DSTDEVP	Calculates the standard deviation based on the entire population of selected database entries
DSUM	Adds the numbers in the field column of records in the database that match the criteria
DVAR	Estimates variance based on a sample from selected database entries
DVARP	Calculates variance based on the entire population of selected database entries

See also "Setting up a criteria range for advanced filtering," in this part, and "Using the Function Wizard," in Part V.

When the comparison involves text, you need to be careful because it may not work the way you think it will. To filter using an exact match to a string, the string must be entered as a formula. For example, to filter using the string *Existing*, enter =**"Existing"**. If you simply enter **Existing**, it does not produce the desired results.

Examples of text criteria are shown as follows.

Criteria	Effect
>K	Text that begins with *L* through *Z*
<>C	All text, except text that begins with *C*
="January"	Text that matches January
Sm*	Text that begins with *Sm*
s*s	Text that begins with *s* and ends with *s*
s?s	Three-letter text that begins with *s* and ends with *s*

Remember: The text comparisons are not case sensitive. For example, si* matches *Simon* as well as *sick*.

Computed criteria filters the list based on one or more calculations and does not use a field header from the list (it uses a new field header). Computed criteria essentially computes a new field for the list so that you must supply new field names in the first row of the criteria range.

Computed criteria is a logical formula (returns True or False) that refers to cells in the first row of data in the list; it does *not* refer to the header row.

See also *MORE Excel 5 For Windows For Dummies* by Greg Harvey, published by IDG Books Worldwide, Inc.

Filtering a list with autofiltering

Autofiltering lets you view only certain rows in your list by hiding rows that do not qualify based on criteria you set.

To autofilter a list

1. Move the cell pointer anywhere within the list.

2. Choose the Data⇨Filter⇨AutoFilter command.

Excel analyzes your list and then adds drop-down arrows to the field names in the header row.

	A	B	C	D	E	F
		Annual	Monthly		Date	
1	Name	Salary	Salary	Location	Hired	
2	James Brackman	42,400	3,533	(All)	2/1/93	
3	Michael Orenthal	28,900	2,408	(Top 10...)	4/5/94	
4	Francis Jenkins	67,800	5,650	(Custom...) Arizona	10/12/93	
5	Peter Yolanda	19,850	1,654	Minnesota	1/4/95	
6	Walter Franklin	45,000	3,750	New York	2/28/90	
7	Louise Victor	52,000	4,333	(Blanks) (NonBlanks)	5/2/94	
8	Sally Rice	48,500	4,042	New York	11/21/92	
9	Charles K. Barkley	24,500	2,042	Minnesota	6/4/90	
10	Melinda Hintquest	56,400	4,700	Arizona	6/1/87	
11	Linda Harper	75,000	6,250	Minnesota	8/7/91	
12	John Daily	87,500	7,292	New York	1/5/93	
13	Elizabeth Becker	89,500	7,458	Arizona	9/29/87	
14						
15						

Employees

3. Click the arrow on one of these drop-down lists.

The list expands to show the unique items in that column.

4. Select an item.

Excel hides all rows except those that include the selected item. In other words, the list is filtered by the item that you selected.

Remember: After you filter the list, the status bar displays a message that tells you how many rows qualified. In addition, the drop-down arrow changes color to remind you that the list is filtered by a value in that column.

The drop-down list includes five other items:

All: Displays all items in the column. Use this to remove filtering for a column.

Top 10: Filters to display the "top 10" items in the list. Actually, you can display any number of the top (or bottom) values.

Custom: Lets you filter the list by multiple items.

Blanks: Filters the list by showing only rows that contain blanks in this column.

NonBlanks: Filters the list by showing only rows that contain non-blanks in this column.

To display the entire list again, select the Data⇨Filter⇨Show All command.

To get out of AutoFilter mode and remove the drop-down arrows from the field names, choose the Data⇨Filter⇨AutoFilter command again.

See also "Performing advanced filtering" and "Filtering a list with custom autofiltering," both in this part.

Filtering a list with custom autofiltering

Normally, autofiltering involves selecting a single value for one or more columns. The list is then filtered by that value. For more flexibility, choose the Custom option in an AutoFilter drop-down list.

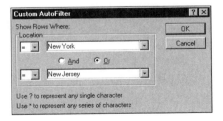

The Custom AutoFilter dialog box lets you filter in several ways:

✦ **Values above or below a specified value:** For example, sales amounts greater than 10,000.

✦ **Values within a range:** For example, sales amounts greater than 10,000 AND sales amounts less than 50,000.

+ **Two discrete values:** For examples, state equal to *New York* OR state equal to *New Jersey.*

+ **Approximate matches:** You can use the * and ? wildcards to filter in many other ways. For example, to display only those customers whose last name begins with a B, use **B***.

Custom autofiltering is useful, but it has limitations. For example, if you would like to filter the list to show only three values in a field (such as New York or New Jersey or Connecticut), you can't do it by using autofiltering. Such filtering tasks require the advanced filtering feature.

See also "Performing advanced filtering," in this part.

Performing advanced filtering

Advanced filtering is more flexible than autofiltering, but it takes some up-front work to use it. Advanced filtering provides you with the following capabilities:

+ You can specify more complex filtering criteria.

+ You can specify computed filtering criteria.

+ You can extract a copy of the rows that meet the criteria to another location.

To perform advanced filtering on a list

1. Set up a criteria range.

2. Choose the Data⇨Filter⇨Advanced Filter command.

3. In the Advanced Filter dialog box, specify the list range and the criteria range, and make sure that the option labeled Filter the List, in-place is selected.

4. Click OK, and the list is filtered by the criteria that you specified.

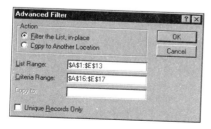

See also "Setting up a criteria range for advanced filtering," in this part.

Setting up a criteria range for advanced filtering

Before you can use the advanced filtering feature, you must set up a *criteria range* — a range on a worksheet that holds the information that Excel uses to filter the list. The criteria range must conform to the following specifications:

✦ The criteria range consists of at least two rows.

✦ The first row contains some or all of the field names from the list.

✦ The other rows consist of filtering criteria.

If you use more than one row below the field names in the criteria range, the criteria in each row are joined with an OR operator.

The entries that you make in a criteria range can be either

✦ **Text or value criteria:** The filtering involves comparisons to a value or text, using operators such as equal (=), greater than (>), not equal to (<>), and so on.

✦ **Computed criteria:** The filtering involves some sort of computation.

Sorting a list

Sorting a list involves rearranging the rows such that they are in ascending or descending order, based on the values in one or more columns. For example, you might want to sort a list of salespeople alphabetically by last name or by sales region. The fastest way to sort a list is to use the Sort Ascending or Sort Descending buttons on the Standard toolbar:

1. Move the cell pointer to the column upon which you want to base the sort.

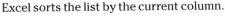 *2.* Click the Sort Ascending button or the Sort Descending button.

Excel sorts the list by the current column.

 If you need to sort by more than one column, repeat the procedure above for each column. Always start with the "least important" column and end with the "most important" column.

 When you sort a filtered list, only the visible rows are sorted. When you remove the filtering from the list, the list will no longer be sorted.

 If the sorted list contains formulas that refer to cells in other rows in the list, the formulas will not be correct after the sorting. If formulas in your list refer to cells outside the list, make sure that the formulas use an absolute cell reference.

Another way to sort a list follows.

1. Choose the Data⇨Sort command.

Excel displays the Sort dialog box.

2. Select the first sort field from the drop-down list labeled Sort By and specify Ascending or Descending order.

3. Repeat Step 2 for the second and third sort fields (if desired).

4. Select any sort options (described below).

First Key Sort Order	Lets you specify a custom sort order for the sort.
Case Sensitive	Makes the sorting case sensitive so that uppercase letters appear before lowercase letters in an ascending sort. Normally, sorting ignores the case of letters.
Orientation	Lets you sort by columns rather than by rows (the default).

5. Click OK and the list's rows are rearranged.

Remember: If the Header Row option is set, the first row (field names) is not affected by the sort.

Sorting a list by more than three fields requires an additional step. If you want to sort your list by five fields (Field1, Field2, Field3, Field4, and Field5), start by sorting by Field3, Field4, and Field5. Then re-sort the list by Field1 and Field2. In other words, sort the three "least important" fields first; they remain in sequence when you do the second sort.

Often, you'll want to keep the records in their original order but perform a temporary sort just to see how it looks. To do so, add an additional column to the list with sequential numbers in it. Then, after you sort, you can return to the original order by re-sorting on the field that has the sequential numbers.

See also "Using a custom sort order," in this part.

Using a custom sort order

Sorting is done either numerically or alphabetically, depending on the data. In some cases, you may want to sort your data in other ways. If your data consists of month names, you probably want them to appear in month order rather than alphabetically. If you sort a list that uses month names, you'll find that this is exactly what happens. Excel, by default, has four custom lists, and you can define your own.

Excel's custom lists are as follows:

✦ **Abbreviated days:** Sun, Mon, Tue, Wed, Thu, Fri, Sat

✦ **Days:** Sunday, Monday, Tuesday, Wednesday, Thursday, Friday, Saturday

✦ **Abbreviated months:** Jan, Feb, Mar, Apr, May, Jun, Jul, Aug, Sep, Oct, Nov, Dec

✦ **Months:** January, February, March, April, May, June, July, August, September, October, November, December

To create a custom list

1. Choose the Tools⇨Options command.

2. In the Options dialog box, click the Custom Lists tab.

3. Click the New List option.

4. Enter your list.

Using an external database

Accessing external database files from Excel is useful when

✦ The database that you need to work with is very large.

✦ The database is shared with others; that is, other users have access to the database and may need to work with the data at the same time.

✦ You want to work with only a subset of the data that meets certain criteria.

✦ The database is in a format that Excel can't read.

After you bring the data into Excel, you can manipulate and format it using any of Excel's commands.

To work with an external database file from Excel, you use the *MS Query* application (which is included with Excel). The general procedure is as follows:

1. Ensure that the MS Query add-in is installed on your system and that the add-in is loaded.

2. Activate a worksheet.

3. Choose the Data⇨Get External Data command to start MS Query.

4. In MS Query, you select the database that you want to use and then create a query — a list of criteria that determines which records you want.

5. Choose Query's File⇨Return Data to Microsoft Excel command.

The data that passes your query is copied to the worksheet, where you can do whatever you like with it.

See also MORE *Excel 5 For Windows For Dummies.*

Goal Seeking: Making a Formula Return a Desired Value

Single-cell goal seeking is a rather simple concept. Excel determines what value in an input cell produces a desired result in a formula cell. Here's the procedure:

1. Start with a workbook that uses formulas.

2. Select the Tools⇨Goal Seek command.

3. Complete the Goal Seek dialog box by specifying the formula cell to change, the value to change it to, and the cell to change.

4. Click OK.

Excel displays the solution.

5. Click OK to replace the original value with the found value; or click Cancel to restore your worksheet to the form that it was in before you issued the Tools⇨Goal Seek command.

Remember: Excel can't always find a value that produces the result that you're looking for (sometimes a solution doesn't exist). In such a case, the Goal Seek status box informs you of that fact. If Excel reports that it can't find a solution, but you're pretty sure that one exists, try these options:

✦ Change the current value of the changing cell to a value closer to the solution and then reissue the command.

✦ Adjust the Maximum Iterations setting in the Calculation panel of the Options dialog box. Increasing the number of iterations makes Excel try other possible solutions.

✦ Double-check your logic and make sure that the formula cell does indeed depend on the specified changing cell.

Performing What-If Analysis (Scenarios)

What-if analysis refers to the process of changing one or more input cells and observing the effects on formulas. An input cell is a cell that is used by a formula. For example, if a formula calculates a monthly payment amount for a loan, the formula would refer to an input cell that contains the loan amount.

Creating a named scenario

Excel's scenario manager feature lets you store different sets of input values (called *changing cells*) for any number of variables and gives a name to each set. You can then select a set of values by name, and Excel displays the worksheet using those values.

To define a scenario

1. Create your worksheet as usual, using input cells that determine the result of one or more formulas.

2. Choose the Tools⇨Scenarios command to display the Scenario Manager dialog box.

3. In the Scenario Manager dialog box, click the Add button to add a scenario.

4. Complete the Add Scenario dialog box (the settings are described as follows).

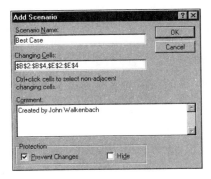

Scenario <u>N</u>ame	The name for the scenario. You can give it any name that you like.
Changing <u>C</u>ells	The input cells for the scenario. You can enter the cell addresses directly or point to them. Multiple selections are allowed, so the input cells do not need to be adjacent. Each named scenario can use the same set of changing cells or different changing cells.
C<u>o</u>mment	By default, Excel displays who created the scenario and the time it was created. You can change this text, add new text to it, or delete it altogether.
Protection	The two options (protecting a scenario and hiding a scenario) are in effect only when the worksheet is protected and the Scenario option is chosen in the Protect Sheet dialog box. Protecting a scenario prevents anyone from modifying it; a hidden scenario doesn't appear in the Scenario Manager dialog box.

5. Click OK to display the Scenario Values dialog box.

6. Enter the values for this scenario in the Scenario Values dialog box.

7. Click the <u>A</u>dd button to add the scenario.

8. Repeat Steps 6 and 7 for each additional scenario.

9. Click Close to close the Scenario Manager dialog box.

The Workgroup toolbar includes a tool named Scenarios, which is a drop-down list box that you can use to display named scenarios. Using this tool may be more efficient than bringing up the Scenario Manager dialog box to view a different scenario.

Remember: The number of changing cells for a scenario is limited to 32.

See also "Creating a scenario summary report," in this part.

Creating a one-input data table

A *one-input data table* displays the results of one or more result formulas for multiple values of a single input cell. For example, if you have a formula that calculates a loan payment, you can create a data table that shows the payment amount for various interest rates. The interest rate cell is the input cell.

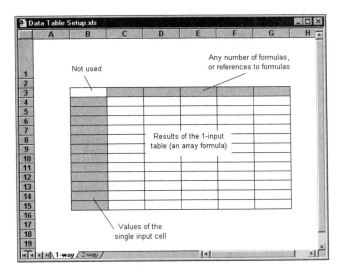

The table below describes how the one-input data table is set up:

Table Area	Description
Left column	Values for the single input cell
Top row	Formulas or references to result formulas elsewhere in the worksheet
Upper-left cell	Not used
Remaining cells	Results entered by Excel

To create the table

1. Select the table range.

2. Choose the Data⇨Table command.

3. Specify the worksheet cell that you're using as the input value.

   If the variables for the input cell are located in a column, use the Column Input Cell field. If the variables are in a row, use the Row Input Cell field.

4. Click OK. Excel performs the calculations and fills in the table.

Remember: Excel uses an array formula that uses the TABLE function. Therefore, the table will be updated if you change the cell references in the first row or plug in different values in the first column.

See also "Creating a two-input data table," in this part.

Creating a scenario summary report

After you've defined at least two scenarios, you can generate reports that summarize the scenarios:

1. Choose the Tools⇔Scenarios command.

2. Click the Summary button in the Scenario Manager dialog box.

3. Select the type of report (described as follows).

- **Scenario Summary:** The summary report is in the form of an outline.

- **Scenario PivotTable:** The summary report is in the form of a pivot table. This gives you more flexibility if you have many scenarios defined with multiple result cells.

4. Specify the summary cells to include in the report.

Excel creates a new worksheet to store the summary table.

See also "Creating a named scenario" and "Pivot Tables," in this part.

Creating a two-input data table

A *two-input data table* displays the results of a single formula for various values of *two* input cells. For example, if you have a formula that calculates a loan payment, you can create a data table that shows the payment amount for various interest rates and loan amounts. The interest rate cell and the loan amount cell are the input cells.

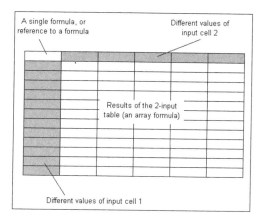

The following table below describes how the two-input data table is set up:

Table Area	Description
Left column	Values for the first input cell
Top row	Values for the second input cell
Upper-left cell	Reference to the single result formula
Remaining cells	Results entered by Excel

To create a two-input data table

1. Select the table range.

2. Choose the Data⇨Table command.

3. Specify the cell for the Row Input Cell.

4. Specify the cell for the Column Input Cell.

5. Click OK.

Excel performs the calculations and fills in the table.

Pivot Tables

A *pivot table* is a dynamic summary of data contained in a database (contained on a worksheet or in an external file). A pivot table lets you create frequency distributions and cross-tabulations of several different data dimensions. In addition, you can display subtotals and any level of detail that you desire.

Generally speaking, fields in a database table can be one of two types:

✦ **Data:** Contains a value.

✦ **Category:** Describes the data.

A database table can have any number of data fields and any number of category fields. When you create a pivot table, you usually want to summarize one or more of the data fields. The values in the category fields appear in the pivot table as rows, columns, or pages.

See also *MORE Excel 5 For Windows For Dummies.*

Creating a pivot table

To create a pivot table from a worksheet database

1. Move the cell pointer to any cell in the database.

2. Choose the Data⇨Pivot Table command. Excel displays the first of four dialog boxes.

3. Make sure that the option labeled Microsoft Excel List or Database is selected and click Next.

4. In the second dialog box, ensure that the database range is specified (Excel will identify the database range automatically) and click Next.

5. The third dialog box shows the field names as buttons. Drag the buttons to an appropriate section of the table layout (PAGE, COLUMN, ROW, or DATA) and click Next.

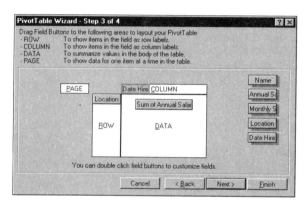

6. In the fourth dialog box, specify options (described below) and click Finish.

Excel creates the pivot table.

Pivot Table Starting Cell	The location for the upper-left cell of the pivot table. If you want the pivot table to be located on a new worksheet, leave this field empty.
Pivot Table Name	You can provide a name for the pivot table. Excel provides default names in the form of PivotTable1, PivotTable2, and so on.
Grand Totals for Columns	Check this box if you want Excel to calculate grand totals for items displayed in columns.
Grand Totals for Rows	Check this box if you want Excel to calculate grand totals for items displayed in rows.
Save Data With Table Layout	If this option is checked, Excel stores an additional copy of the data (called a *pivot table cache*) to allow it to recalculate the table more quickly when you change the layout.
AutoFormat Table	Check this box if you want Excel to apply one of its AutoFormats to the pivot table. Excel uses the AutoFormat even if you rearrange the table layout.

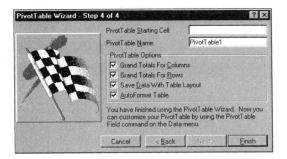

See also "Using AutoFormats," in Part III.

If the data is in an external database, select the External Data Source option in Step 3, above. The data is retrieved using Query (a separate application), and you'll be prompted for the data source in the second PivotTable Wizard dialog box.

See also "Using an external database," in this part.

Remember: In Step 5, you can drag as many field buttons as you want to any of the table locations, and you don't have to use all the fields. Fields that aren't used don't appear in the pivot table.

Formatting a pivot table

When you create a pivot table, you have an option of applying a table AutoFormat. After the pivot table is created, you can specify a different AutoFormat. Often, the number format used in an AutoFormat is not appropriate for the data.

If you change the number and then apply an AutoFormat using the option to ignore number formatting, Excel *still* uses the AutoFormat's number format when the pivot table is refreshed.

If you want to use a different number format for the data, here's what you need to do:

1. Select any cell in the pivot table's data area.

2. Right-click and choose Pivot Table Field from the shortcut menu.

Excel displays its Pivot Table Field dialog box.

3. Click the Number button.

4. Select the number format that you need.

If you use this procedure, the number format "sticks" even after the pivot table is refreshed.

Grouping pivot table items

A handy feature enables you to group specific items in a field of a pivot table. If one of the fields in your database consists of dates, for example, the pivot table displays a separate row or column for every date. You may find it more useful to group the dates into months or quarters and then hide the details.

To create a group of items in a pivot table

1. Select the cells to be grouped.

2. Choose the Data⇨Group and Outline⇨Group command.

Excel creates a new field that consists of the selected items.

3. You can change the names of the new field and the items by editing them.

If the items to be grouped are not next to each other, make a multiple selection by pressing Ctrl and selecting the items that will make up the group.

If the field items consist of values, dates, or times, you can let Excel do the grouping for you. To create groups *automatically*

1. Select any item in the field (only one).

2. Choose the Data⇨Group and Outline⇨Group command.

Excel displays the Grouping dialog box.

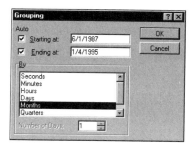

3. Select the grouping options.

4. Click OK.

Excel creates the groups.

Inserting a new field into a pivot table

To add a new field to a pivot table

1. Move the cell pointer anywhere within the pivot table.

2. Choose the Data⇨Pivot Table command.

Excel displays the third dialog box from the Pivot Table Wizard.

3. Drag the new field to the desired location in the pivot table diagram.

4. Click Finish and Excel updates the pivot table with the new field or fields that you added.

Modifying a pivot table's structure

A pivot table displayed in a worksheet includes the field buttons. You can drag any of the field buttons to a new position in the pivot table (this is known as *pivoting*). For example, you can drag a column field to the row position. Excel immediately redisplays the pivot table to reflect your change.

TIP

You also can change the order of the row fields or the column fields by dragging the buttons. This affects how the fields are nested and can have a dramatic effect on how the table looks.

Remember: A pivot table is a special type of range, and (with a few exceptions) you can't make any changes to it. For example, you can't insert or delete rows, edit results, or move cells. If you attempt to do so, Excel displays an error message.

Refreshing a pivot table

If you change the source data that is used by a pivot table, the pivot table doesn't get updated automatically. Rather, you must "refresh" it manually. To refresh a pivot table, use any of the these methods:

✦ Choose the Data⇨Refresh Data command.

✦ Right-click anywhere in the pivot table and select Refresh Data from the shortcut menu.

✦ Click the Refresh button on the Query and Pivot toolbar.

Remember: If the source database is large, there may be some delay while this recalculation takes place, but for small databases the update is virtually instantaneous.

Removing a field from a pivot table

To remove a field from a pivot table

1. Click the field button that you want to remove.

2. Drag it away from the pivot table.

3. Release the mouse button, and the table is updated to exclude the field.

Using the Analysis ToolPak Add-In

The Analysis ToolPak is an add-in that provides analytical capability that normally isn't available in Excel. The Analysis ToolPak consists of two parts:

✦ 19 analytical procedures

✦ 93 built-in worksheet functions

These analytical tools offer many features useful to the scientific, engineering, and educational communities, as well as business users.

If the Tools⇨Data Analysis command is not available on your system, you need to attach the add-in. To make the Analysis ToolPak tools available

1. Select the Tools⇨Add-Ins command.

2. Place a check mark next to the Analysis ToolPak add-in.

3. Click OK to make the Analysis ToolPak available whenever you start Excel.

Remember: If the Analysis ToolPak doesn't appear in the list of add-ins, you'll need to rerun the Setup program for Excel (or Microsoft Office) and choose the Custom option. This lets you copy the files used by the Analysis ToolPak to your hard drive.

Using the Analysis ToolPak procedures

The procedures in the Analysis ToolPak add-in are relatively straight-forward. Here are the general steps you use:

1. Select the Tools⇨Data Analysis command, which displays the Data Analysis ToolPak dialog box.

2. Scroll through the list until you find the analysis tool that you want to use.

3. Click OK and you get a new dialog box that's specific to the procedure you selected.

Normally, you need to specify one or more input ranges (the data to be analyzed), plus an output range that will hold the results (one cell will do). Alternatively, you can specify that the results be placed on a new worksheet or in a new workbook. The procedures vary in the amount of additional information required.

Remember: An option that you'll see in many of the dialog boxes displayed by the Analysis ToolPak is whether or not your data range includes labels. If so, you can specify the entire range, including the labels, and indicate to Excel that the first column (or row) contains labels. Excel then uses these labels in the tables it produces.

Using the Analysis ToolPak worksheet functions

The Analysis ToolPak functions appear in the Function Wizard in the following categories:

- ✦ Date and Time

- ✦ Engineering (a new category that appears when the Analysis ToolPak is installed)

- ✦ Financial

- ✦ Information

- ✦ Math & Trig

Remember: If you attempt to use any of the Analysis ToolPak functions when the add-in is not loaded, the formula will display #NAME?

Part VII

Charting, Mapping, and Drawing

This part deals with topics related to creating charts and maps, both of which can help you visualize spreadsheet data. It also covers Excel's drawing tools, which you can use to draw diagrams directly on a worksheet.

In this part . . .

🖊 **Creating and customizing charts**

🖊 **Creating and customizing maps**

🖊 **Using Excel's drawing tools**

Charting

Before you can do anything with a chart, you must activate it:

+ To activate a chart on a chart sheet: Click the chart sheet's tab.

+ To activate an embedded chart: Double-click the chart.

Adding a new data series to a chart

There are several ways to add a new data series to a chart:

+ Select the range to be added and drag it into the chart. When you release the mouse button, Excel updates the chart with the data you dragged into it. This technique works only if the chart is embedded on the worksheet.

+ Activate the chart and select the Insert⇨New Data command. Excel displays a dialog box that prompts you for the range of data to add to the chart.

+ Select the range to be added and copy it to the Clipboard. Then activate the chart and choose the Edit⇨Paste Special command. Excel responds with the Paste Special dialog box. Complete this dialog box to correspond to the data that you selected.

+ Activate the chart and then click the ChartWizard tool. You'll get the first ChartWizard dialog box. Edit the range reference to include the new data series (or point to the new range in the worksheet). Click Finish and Excel updates the chart with the new data.

Adding a trendline to a data series

When you're plotting data over time, you may want to plot a *trend-line* that points out general trends in your data. In some cases, you also can forecast future data with trendlines:

1. Activate the chart.

2. Select the data series.

3. Choose the Insert⇨Trendline command.

4. In the Type panel of the Trendline dialog box, choose the type of trendline you want.

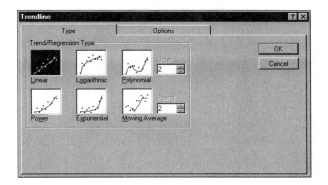

You can also set options by clicking the Options tab.

The Options tab enables you to specify a name to appear in the
legend and the number of periods that you want to forecast. Two
additional options enable you to specify that the equation used for
the trendline and the R^2 value appear on the chart.

Remember: When Excel inserts a trendline, it may look like a new
data series, but it's not. The trendline is a new chart element with a
name, such as S2T1 (series 2, trendline 1). You can double-click a
trendline to change its formatting.

Adding error bars to a data series

For certain chart types, you can add *error bars* to indicate "plus or
minus" information that reflects uncertainty in the data. Error bars
are appropriate only for area, bar, column, line, and XY charts:

1. Activate the chart.

2. Select the data series.

3. Choose the Format⇨Selected Data Series command.

4. In the Format Data Series dialog box, click the Y Error Bars tab.

5. Select the type of error bar you want.

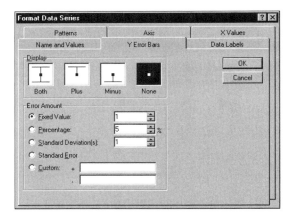

The error bar choices are

Fixed Value	The error bars are fixed by an amount you specify.
Percentage	The error bars are a percentage of each value.
Standard Deviation(s)	The error bars are in the number of standard deviation units that you specify. (Excel calculates the standard deviation of the data series.)
Standard Error	The error bars are one standard error unit. (Excel calculates the standard error of the data series.)
Custom	You set the error bar units for the upper or lower error bars. You can either enter a value or a range reference that holds the error values that you want to plot as error bars.

Remember: A data series in an XY chart can have error bars for both the X values and Y values.

Changing a chart's data series

Often, you create a chart that uses a particular range of data, and then you extend the data range by adding new data points in the worksheet. When you add new data to a range, the new data won't be included in the data series. Or you may delete some of the data points in a range that is plotted. If you delete data from a range, the chart displays the deleted data as zero values.

To update the chart to reflect the new data range

1. Activate the chart.

2. Select the data series.

3. Choose the Format⇨Selected Data Series command.

4. In the Format Data Series dialog box, select the tab labeled Name and Values.

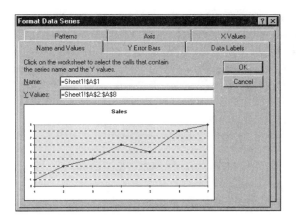

5. Edit the formula so that it refers to the range you want to use in the chart (or select the <u>Y</u> Values box and point to the new range in the worksheet).

6. Click OK, and the chart is updated with the new data range.

A better way to handle data ranges that change is to use named ranges. Simply create names for the data ranges that you use in the chart. Activate the chart, select the data series, and edit the SERIES formula. Replace each range reference with the corresponding range name. If you change the definition for a name, the chart is updated.

Changing a chart's scale

Adjusting the scale of a value axis can have a dramatic effect on the appearance of the chart. Excel always determines the scale for your charts automatically. You can, however, override Excel's choice:

1. Activate the chart.

2. Select the axis.

3. Choose the F<u>o</u>rmat⇨Selected Axis command.

4. In the Format Axis dialog box, click the Scale tab.

5. Make the changes.

Remember: The dialog box varies slightly depending on which axis is selected.

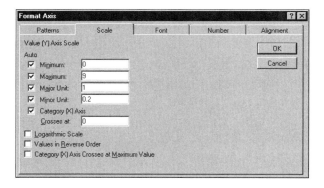

The Format Axis dialog box offers the following options:

Minimum: Lets you enter a minimum value for the axis. If checked, Excel determines this value automatically.

Maximum: Lets you enter a maximum value for the axis. If checked, Excel determines this value automatically.

Major Unit: Lets you enter the number of units between major tick marks. If checked, Excel determines this value automatically.

Minor Unit: Lets you enter the number of units between minor tick marks. If checked, Excel determines this value automatically.

Axis Type **Axis Crosses at:** Lets you position the axes at a different location. By default, the axes are positioned at the edge of the plot area. The exact wording of this option varies, depending on which axis you select.

Logarithmic Scale: Lets you use a logarithmic scale for the axes. Useful for scientific applications in which the values to be plotted have an extremely large range, a log scale gives you an error message if the scale includes 0 or negative values.

Values in Reverse Order: Makes the scale values extend in the opposite direction.

Axis Type **Crosses at Maximum Value:** Lets you position the axes at the maximum value of the perpendicular axis (normally, the axis is positioned at the minimum value). The exact wording varies, depending on which axis you select.

Changing a chart's gridlines

Gridlines can help you determine what the chart series represents numerically. Gridlines simply extend the tick marks on the axes.

To add or remove gridlines

1. Activate the chart.

2. Choose the Insert⇨Gridlines command.

3. Check or uncheck the check boxes that correspond to the desired gridlines.

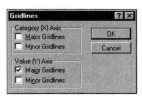

Remember: Each axis has two sets of gridlines: major and minor. Major units are the ones displaying a label. Minor units are those in between. If you're working with a 3-D chart, the dialog box has options for three sets of gridlines.

To modify the properties of a set of gridlines

1. Activate the chart.

2. Select one gridline in the set.

3. Choose the Format⇨Selected Gridlines command.

4. In the Format Gridlines dialog box, select the Patterns tab to change the line style, width, and color.

5. In the Format Gridlines dialog box ,select the Scale tab to make adjustments to the scale used on the axis.

See also "Changing a chart's scale," in this part.

Changing the chart type

Excel supports a wide variety of chart types (line charts, column charts, and so on).

To change the chart type

1. Activate the chart.

2. Click the drop-down arrow of the Chart Type tool on the Chart toolbar. The tool expands to show all 15 basic chart types.

3. Click the desired chart type.

You can also

1. Choose the Format⇨AutoFormat command, which displays the AutoFormat dialog box.

2. Select the Built-In option.

The Galleries box displays the names of the chart categories (plus a Combination chart type). Selecting a chart type displays the various AutoFormats for the selected chart type.

3. Choose an AutoFormat and click OK. The chart changes to the type you selected.

You also can use the Format⇨Chart Type command to change a chart's type. This command lets you change the type of the entire chart or just a data series. If you want to make one series a column chart and another series a line chart, you can do it in the Chart Type dialog box. Select the series that you want to change and then choose the Selected Series option.

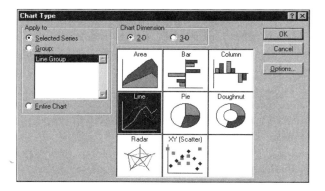

If you've customized some aspects of your chart, choosing a new AutoFormat may override some or all of the changes you've made. For example, if you've added gridlines to the chart and then select an AutoFormat that doesn't use gridlines, your gridlines disappear.

Changing the default chart type

Excel's default chart type is a 2-D column chart with a light-gray plot area, a legend (which describes the data series) on the right, and horizontal gridlines. If you don't like the looks of this chart, or if you normally use a different type of chart, you can easily change the default chart. To do so

1. Create a chart with the characteristics that you want in your default chart.

2. Activate the chart.

3. Choose the Tools⇨Options command.

4. Click the Chart tab in the options dialog box.

5. Click the Use the Current Chart button.

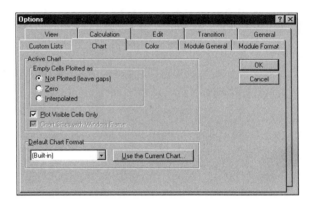

If you've defined any custom AutoFormats, you can pick one of them from the list; it will then become the new default chart.

If you have many charts of the same type to create, it's much more efficient to change the default chart format to the chart type with which you're working. Then you can create all of your charts without using the ChartWizard.

Creating a custom chart AutoFormat

Excel has more than 100 predefined chart AutoFormats. You can also create your own custom AutoFormats. Like the predefined AutoFormats, a custom AutoFormat can be applied to any chart:

1. Create a chart that's customized the way you want.

For example, you can set any of the colors or line styles, change the scales, modify fonts and type sizes, add gridlines, add a title, and even add free-floating text or graphic images.

2. Choose Format⇨AutoFormat.

3. In the AutoFormat dialog box, select the User-Defined option in the Formats Used group box.

4. To create a new AutoFormat based on the current chart, click the Customize button in the AutoFormat dialog box, which displays another dialog box.

5. To add your new AutoFormat, click the Add button in the User-Defined AutoFormats dialog box, which brings up yet another dialog box.

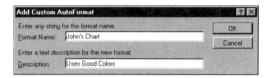

6. In the Add Custom AutoFormat dialog box, type a name for the AutoFormat in the top text box and a description in the bottom text box.

7. Click OK to return to the User-Defined AutoFormats dialog box, and then click the Close button to return to your chart.

The AutoFormat name that you supplied now appears whenever you choose the Format⫘AutoFormat command and click the User-Defined option.

Creating a default chart on a chart sheet

To quickly create a chart on a new chart sheet

1. Select the worksheet data to be charted.

2. Press F11.

Excel inserts a new chart sheet and displays the chart based on the selected data. Excel created its default chart type using the default settings.

Remember: For more control over the chart-making process, use the ChartWizard.

In some cases, Excel can't determine how to chart the selected data — for example, if the range doesn't include any text, Excel can't determine whether the chart should plot rows or columns. In such a case, Excel starts the ChartWizard so that you can clarify your intentions.

See also "Using the ChartWizard," in this part.

Creating a picture chart

Excel lets you replace bars, columns, or line chart markers with pictures (graphic images). You can only paste pictures into four chart types: columns, bars, lines, and XY (2-D charts only).

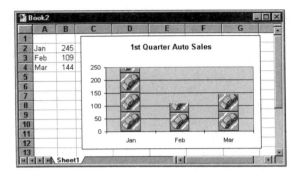

To create a picture chart

1. Create a chart as usual (it must be a bar, column, or line chart).

2. Locate the graphic image that you want to use and copy it to the Clipboard (the technique will vary, depending on the application).

You may want to paste it into Excel first, where you can adjust the size, remove the borders, and add a background color.

3. Activate the chart.

4. Select the data series.

5. Choose the Edit➪Paste command.

Remember: Column and bar charts with pictures pasted in them have a different Patterns panel in their Format Data Series dialog box. The panel gives you some options that affect how the image appears. For example, you can stretch or stack the images in a column chart.

Deleting a chart element or data series

Most (but not all) elements in a chart can be deleted.

To delete a chart element

1. Select the element or data series to be deleted.

2. Press Delete.

See also "Selecting a chart element," in this part.

Remember: If you delete the last data series in a chart, the chart will be empty.

Displaying data labels in a chart

Sometimes, you want your chart to display the actual data values for each point on the chart. Or, you may want to display the category label for each data point.

To add data labels to a chart series

1. Activate the chart.

2. Select the data series.

3. Choose the Format⇨Selected Data Series command.

4. In the Format Data Series dialog box, click the Data Labels tab.

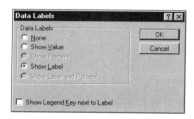

5. Select the option that corresponds to the type of data labels that you want.

Remember: The data labels are linked to the worksheet, so if your data changes, the labels also change. If you would like to override the data label with some other text, select the label and enter the new text (or even a cell reference) in the formula bar.

If the data labels aren't positioned properly, you can select an individual label and move it to a better location by dragging it.

Remember: It is not possible to specify a range of text to be used as data labels. You must add data labels and then edit each one manually.

Embedding a chart with the ChartWizard

To invoke the ChartWizard to create an embedded chart

1. Select the data to be charted.

2. Click the ChartWizard button on the Standard toolbar (or, choose the Insert⇨Chart⇨On This Sheet command).

The mouse pointer changes to a miniature chart.

3. Click and drag in the worksheet to delineate the chart's size and position.

4. Make your choices in the ChartWizard dialog boxes.

5. In the final ChartWizard dialog box, click Finish.

Excel creates the chart you specified.

See also "Using the ChartWizard," in this part.

Handling missing data in a chart

Sometimes, data that you're charting may be missing one or more data points. Excel offers several options for handling the missing data:

1. Activate the chart.

2. Choose the Tools⇨Options command.

3. In the Options dialog box, click the Chart tab.

4. Select the option that corresponds to how you want to handle the missing data.

The options are as follows:

- **Not Plotted (leave gaps):** Missing data is simply ignored, and the data series will have a gap for each missing data point.

- **Zero:** Missing data is treated as zero.

- **Interpolated:** Missing data is calculated using data on either side of the missing point(s).

Remember: The options that you set apply to the entire active chart; you can't set a different option for different series in the same chart.

Modifying a chart element

Most elements in a chart can be modified in several ways. For example, you can change colors, line widths, fonts, and so on. Modifications are made in the Format dialog box (which varies for each type of chart element).

To modify an element in a chart

1. Select the chart element.

2. Access the Format dialog box using any of the following techniques:

- Double-click the item.

- Choose the Format [*Item Name*] command.

- Press Ctrl+1.

- Right-click the item and choose Format [*Item Name*] from the shortcut menu.

3. Click the tab that corresponds to what you want to do.

4. Make the changes.

5. Click OK.

See also "Selecting a chart element," in this part.

Moving a chart element

Some of the chart parts can be moved (any of the titles and the legend). To move a chart element

1. Select the chart element.

2. Drag the element to the desired location in the chart.

See also "Selecting a chart element," in this part.

Printing charts

There's nothing special about printing embedded charts; it works just like printing a worksheet. As long as the embedded chart is included in the range to be printed, the chart will be printed as it appears on-screen.

Remember: If you print in Draft mode, embedded charts won't be printed.

If you don't want a particular embedded chart to appear on your printout

1. Right-click the chart.

2. Choose Format Object from the Shortcut menu.

3. Activate the Properties tab in the Format Object dialog box.

4. Remove the check mark from the Print Object check box.

If the chart is on a chart sheet, it prints on a page by itself. If you access Excel's Page Setup dialog box when the chart sheet is active, you'll find that the Sheet tab is replaced with a tab named Chart.

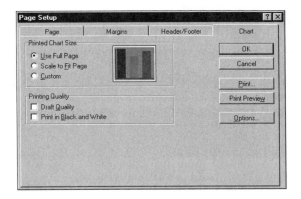

This dialog box has several options:

Use Full Page: The chart will be printed to the full width and height of the page margins. This is usually not a good choice because the chart's relative proportions will change and you lose the WYSIWYG (what you see is what you get) advantage.

Scale To Fit Page: This option expands the chart proportionally in both dimensions until one dimension fills the space between the margins. This option usually results in the best printout.

Custom: This option prints the chart as it appears on your screen. Use the View⇨Sized with Window command to make the chart correspond to the window size and proportions. The chart prints at the current window size and proportions.

Choosing the Print in Black and White option prints the data series with black and white patterns rather than colors.

Rotating 3-D charts

When you work with 3-D charts, you may find that some data is completely or partially obscured. You can rotate the chart so that it shows the data better:

1. Activate the 3-D chart.

2. Choose the Format⇨3-D View command.

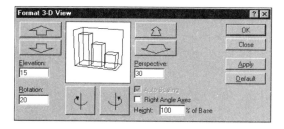

3. In the Format 3-D View dialog box, make your rotations and perspective changes by clicking the appropriate controls.

4. Click OK (or click Apply to see the changes without closing the dialog box).

You can also rotate the chart in real time by dragging corners with the mouse.

Selecting a chart element

Modifying an element in a chart is similar to everything else you do in Excel: First you make a selection (in this case, select a chart part), and then you issue a command to do something with the selection.

Once you activate a chart, you can select a chart element in either of two ways:

+ Click the chart element.

+ Press the up-arrow or down-arrow key to cycle through all parts in the chart. When a data series is selected, you can press the right-arrow or left-arrow key to select individual points in the series.

In either case, the name of the selected item appears in the Name box (at the left of the formula bar). Many of the chart element names include a number that further describes the part. For example, the first axis in a chart is named Axis 1, the second is Axis 2, and so on.

The following table lists the various elements of a chart (not all of these parts appear in every chart).

Part	Description
Axis *n*	One of the chart's axes. For example, the value axis is Axis 1.
Chart	The chart's background.
Corners	The corners of a 3-D chart (except 3-D pie charts). Select the corners if you want to rotate a 3-D chart using a mouse.
Dropline *n*	A dropline that extends from the data point downward to the axis. For example, the first dropline is Dropline 1.

Part	Description
Floor	The floor of a 3-D chart (except 3-D pie charts).
Gridline *n*	A chart can have major and minor gridlines for each axis. For example, the major gridline for the value axis is Gridline 1.
HiLoline *n*	A high-line in a stock market chart. For example, the first HiLoline is HiLoline 1.
Legend	The chart's legend (which describes the data series).
Legend Entry *n*	One of the text entries inside of a legend. For example, the first item in the legend is Legend Entry 1.
Legend Key *n*	One of the keys inside of a legend. For example, the key for the first item in the legend is Legend Key 1.
Plot	The chart's plot area — the actual chart, without the legend.
Seriesline *n*	A line that connects series. For example, the first series line is Seriesline 1.
S*n*	A data series. For example, the first data series is S1.
S*n*E	Error bars for a series. For example, the error bar for the first data series is S1E.
S*n*P*k*	A point in a data series. For example, the second point in the first data series is S1P2.
S*n*T*k*	A trendline for a data series. For example, the first trendline for the first data series is S1T1.
Text Axis *n*	An axis label. For example, the label for the value axis is Text Axis 1.
Text S*n*	Data labels for a series. For example, Text S1 are data labels for the first series.
Text S*n*P*k*	A data label for a point in a series. For example, the data label for the second point in the first data series is S1P2.
Title	The chart's title.
Upbar *n*	A bar in a stock market chart. For example, the first Upbar is Upbar 1.
Walls	The walls of a 3-D chart only (except 3-D pie charts).

Using the ChartWizard

The ChartWizard consists of a series of five dialog boxes that prompt you for various settings for the chart. By the time you reach the last dialog box, the chart will usually be just what you need:

1. Before you invoke the ChartWizard, you should select the data that will be included in the chart. Include in your selection items such as labels and series identifiers.

The data that you're plotting doesn't have to be contiguous. You can press Ctrl while making a multiple selection.

 2. After selecting the data, invoke the ChartWizard by clicking the ChartWizard button on the Standard toolbar.

Remember: If you want to create a chart on a new sheet, use the Insert⇨Chart⇨As New Sheet command.

3. Identify the area for the chart.

When you first invoke the ChartWizard, the mouse pointer changes shape (small cross and a miniature chart). Click and drag in the worksheet to delineate the approximate size and rough location of the embedded chart. Release the mouse button and Excel displays the first ChartWizard dialog box. The chart won't be created until the ChartWizard finishes.

Remember: If you're creating a chart on a new sheet, don't specify the chart size and position.

ChartWizard Step 1 of 5

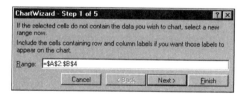

1. Verify that the dialog box displays the correct data range.

If you selected a range of cells before invoking the ChartWizard, that range's address appears in the Range box. Otherwise, specify the range that contains the data to be charted.

2. Click the Next button to move on to the next step.

ChartWizard Step 2 of 5

In the second step of the ChartWizard, specify the general chart type that you want to create. You have 15 types from which to choose, displayed as icons (these images don't represent your actual data).

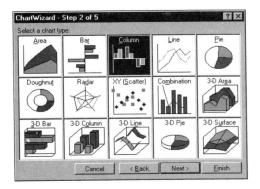

Select a chart type and click Next.

Remember: While using the ChartWizard, you can go back to the previous step by clicking the <u>B</u>ack button. Or, you can click <u>F</u>inish to end the ChartWizard. If you end it early, Excel creates the chart using the information you provided up to that point.

ChartWizard Step 3 of 5

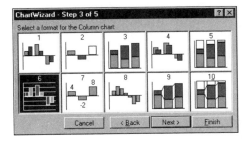

The third ChartWizard dialog box varies depending on your choice in the previous dialog box. This step shows all available AutoFormats for the chart type that you selected. Choose the AutoFormat that you want and click Next.

ChartWizard Step 4 of 5

Step 4 of the ChartWizard displays the chart using the actual data and also lets you modify (or verify) Excel's choices in creating the chart. The options depend on the chart type that you selected. If you change any of these options, the chart displayed in the dialog box is updated so that you can see the effects of your changes.

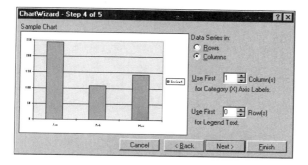

Remember: The Data Series in option in this dialog box deals with the orientation of the data (arranged in rows or columns). This is a very critical choice that has a drastic effect on the look of your chart. Most of the time, Excel guesses correctly — but not always.

ChartWizard Step 5 of 5

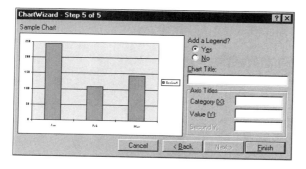

The final ChartWizard dialog box lets you add various text elements to the chart: a legend, title, and titles for the axes. Again, the displayed chart is updated so that you can see the changes as you make them.

Remember: If you didn't select cells that contained series labels when you started, Excel uses "dummy" names if you select the legend option. For example, the first series appears as Series 1, the second as Series 2, and so on.

When you're satisfied with the chart that appears in the dialog box, click Finish. Excel creates the chart using the options that you specified.

Working with chart legends

If you created your chart with the ChartWizard, you had an option to include a legend. If you change your mind, you can easily delete the legend or add one if you need one.

If you didn't include legend text when you originally selected the cells to create the chart, Excel displays *Series 1, Series 2*, and so on in the legend. To add series names

1. Select the chart series.

2. Choose the Format⇨Selected Data Series command.

3. In the Format Data Series dialog box, click the Name and Values tab.

4. In the Name box, enter a cell reference that contains the label or enter a label formula directly (for example, =**"First Quarter"**).

Mapping

Creating maps from worksheet data using Excel's Data Map feature is often an excellent way to present a large amount of data that is categorized by geography.

Remember: When a map is activated, Excel's menus and toolbars are replaced by Data Map's menus and toolbar. When you click outside of the map, Excel's user interface is restored.

Adding and removing map features

To add or remove certain features of a map

1. Double-click the Map button on the toolbar to activate the map.

2. Select the Map⇨Features command

3. In the Map Features dialog box, turn a feature *on* by placing a check mark next to it. Turn a feature *off* by removing the check mark.

4. Click OK to update the chart.

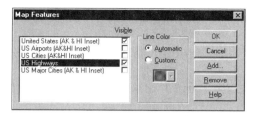

Remember: The features available vary with the map that you're using. If a feature isn't on the list, add it by clicking the Add button.

The table below lists the features available for each map. You can, however, add features from different maps (add world oceans to a map of North America, for instance).

Map	Features
Australia	Airports, Cities, Highways, Major Cities
Canada	Airports, Cities, Forward Sortation Areas, Highways, Lakes, Major Cities
Europe	Airports, Cities, Highways, Major Cities
Mexico	Cities, Highways, Major Cities
UK	2-Digit Post Codes, Airports, Cities, Highways, Major Cities, Standard Regions
US in North America	5-Digit Zip Code Centers, Highways, Major Cities, Great Lakes
US (AK & HI Inset)	Airports, Cities, Major Cities
World	Capitals, Countries, Graticule (lines of latitude and longitude), Oceans

Adding labels and text to a map

Normally, a map doesn't have labels to identify areas. You can't add labels to all areas automatically (for example, all states in the U.S.), but you can add individual labels one at a time. You also can insert data values that correspond to a particular map region (such as sales for New Jersey).

To add a label to a map

1. Click the Label tool.

2. In the Map Labels dialog box, select an option:

Map feature names	This option inserts labels for the various parts of the map (for example, state names in a U.S. map).
Values from	This option lets you insert data values from a category in the list box.

3. Click OK.

4. After closing the dialog box, drag the mouse pointer over the map.

The label or data value appears when the mouse pointer is over a map region.

5. Click to place the label or data value.

To move a label, click and drag it to a new location. You can change the font, size, or color of a label by double-clicking it. Stretching the label (by dragging a border) also makes the font larger or smaller.

To add free-floating text to your map

1. Click the Text tool.

2. Click the area of the map where you want to add text.

3. Enter your text.

Adding new data to a map

After you've created a map, you can add more data to it. Use the Insert⇨Data command to add data from a worksheet range or use the Insert⇨External Data command to add new data from a database file.

Remember: Make sure that the data includes geographic labels that match the map to which you're adding data.

Creating a map

To create a map

1. Select the data to be mapped.

This must be one column of area names and at least one column of data. If the columns have descriptive headers, include these in the selection.

 2. Choose the Insert⇨Map command (or click the Map button on the Standard toolbar).

3. Click and drag in the worksheet to specify the location and size of the map.

4. If two or more maps are possible (or if you've developed any custom map templates), you get a dialog box that lets you select the desired map from this list.

Data Map analyzes the area labels and generates the appropriate map.

Remember: Unlike charts, maps must be embedded in a worksheet (there are no separate "map sheets").

To order additional maps or data from MapInfo (the company that developed Data Map), you can contact the company directly. For information on how to do so, activate a map and click the Help⇨About command.

Modifying a map legend

A map displays a separate legend for each map format that it uses. To modify a legend, double-click it. The Edit Legend dialog box appears, and you can make the following selections.

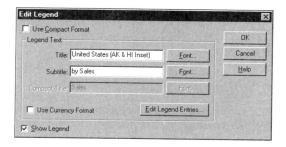

Compact Format: This option determines the size of the legend. A compact legend takes up less space, but it doesn't give many details.

Title: Text that appears at the top of the legend.

Subtitle: Text that appears below the title.

Compact Title: Text that appears when the Compact format option is selected.

Font: Clicking this button lets you adjust the font used.

Edit Legend Entries: Clicking this button lets you edit the labels used in the legend.

Show Legend: This check box determines whether the legend is visible or not.

Setting the map format (s)

 When a map first appears, the Data Map Control dialog box is visible. This dialog box is used to change the format of the selected map (use the Show/Hide Map Control tool to toggle the display of this dialog box).

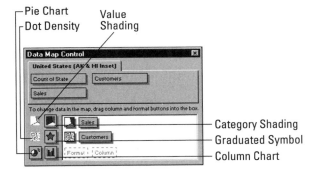

Following are descriptions of each map format.

Value Shading: Each map region is shaded, based on the value of its data. This format is appropriate for quantitative information such as sales, population, and so on.

Category Shading: Each map region is colored based on a data value. The map legend has one entry (color) for every value of the data range. Therefore, this format is appropriate for data that has a small number of discrete values.

Dot Density: This format displays data as a series of dots. Larger values translate into more dots (the dots are placed randomly within a map region).

Graduated Symbol: This format displays a symbol, the size of which is proportional to the area's data value.

Pie Chart: This map format requires at least two columns of data. Maps with this format display a pie chart within each map region.

Column Chart: This map format requires at least two columns of data. It's similar to the pie chart format, except that it displays a column chart instead of a pie chart.

By default, maps are created using the Value Shading map format. You can change the format to display two or more formats on a single map.

Remember: A single map can include multiple formats for different data. You do this by stacking groups of icons and data fields in the Data Map Control dialog box.

The top of the dialog box displays all of the available data fields (which correspond to the columns that you selected when you created the map). The bottom part contains the map format information.

Six format icons on the left determine the map format. Combine a map format icon with one or more data fields by dragging. Some map formats use more than one data field. In such a case, you can drag additional data fields next to the icon.

To change options for a particular map format, use either of these techniques:

✦ Double-click the format icon.

✦ Use the <u>M</u>ap menu and choose the menu item appropriate for the format that you want to change.

Either way, you get a dialog box appropriate to the map format.

Setting up data to be mapped

The Data Map feature works with data stored in a list format. The first column of the list should be map region names (such as states or countries). The columns to the right should be data for each area. You can have any number of data columns because you select which columns to use after the map is created.

See also "Creating a map," in this part.

Updating a map

If you change any of the data used in a map, the map displays an exclamation point in its upper-left corner. Click this icon to re-draw the map using the updated data.

Drawing

Drawing objects with the drawing tools is quite intuitive:

1. Make sure the Drawing toolbar is displayed.

If it's not, click the Drawing button on the toolbar or choose the View⇨Toolbars command and place a check next to the Drawing option in the Toolbars list.

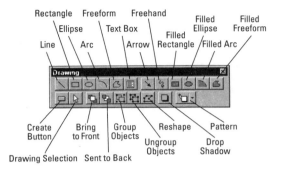

2. Click the appropriate drawing tool.

3. Drag in the worksheet to create the shape (the mouse pointer changes shape, reminding you that you're drawing an object).

4. Release the mouse button. The object is drawn and selected, and its name appears in the Name box.

You can control how objects appear in the View tab of the Options dialog box. Normally, the Show All option is selected. You can hide all objects by choosing Hide All or display objects as placeholders by selecting Show Placeholders (this may speed things up if you have complex objects that take a long time to redraw).

To create a perfect square, press Shift while you draw a rectangle. Similarly, pressing Shift while you draw an ellipse gives you a perfect circle. To constrain a line or arrow object to angles that are divisible by 45 degrees, press Shift while you draw the object.

To make an object line up precisely to the worksheet row and column gridlines, press the Alt key while you draw the object.

Remember: By default, drawn objects are printed along with the worksheet. If you don't want the objects to print, you have two options:

+ Access the Sheet panel of the Page Setup dialog box and select the Draft Quality option.

+ Right-click the object, select Format Object from the shortcut menu and uncheck the Print Object check box in the Properties panel.

Remember: To use Excel's drawing tools, you must display the Drawing toolbar. The drawing objects feature is one of the few features in Excel that's not available from the menus.

Changing the stack order of drawn objects

As you add drawn objects to the draw layer of a worksheet, you'll find that objects are "stacked" on top of each other in the order in which you add them. New objects are stacked on top of older objects.

If you find that an object is obscuring part of another, you can change the order in this stack:

1. Select an object by clicking it once.

 2. Click the Bring to Front tool on the Drawing toolbar to move the object to the top of the stack.

 3. Click on the Send to Back tool to move the object to the bottom of the stack.

You also can use Format⇨Placement or the shortcut menu.

Controlling how objects interact with cells

Objects placed on the draw layer of a worksheet can be moved, resized, copied, and deleted — with no effect on any other elements in the worksheet.

Objects on the draw layer have properties that relate to how they are moved and sized when underlying cells are moved and sized. To change an object's properties

1. Select the object by clicking it once.

2. Choose the Format⇨Object command.

3. Click the Properties tab in the Format Object dialog box.

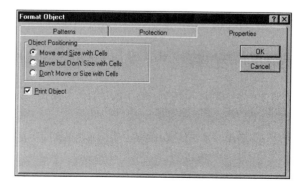

4. Select the appropriate option button (as described below) and click OK.

Move and <u>S</u>ize with Cells	If selected, the object appears to be attached to the cells beneath it. For example, if you insert rows above the object, the object moves down. If you increase the column width, the object gets wider.
<u>M</u>ove but Don't Size with Cells	If selected, the object moves if rows or columns are inserted, but it never changes its size if you change row heights or column widths.
<u>D</u>on't Move or Size with Cells	If selected, the object will be completely independent of the underlying cells.

Excel also lets you *attach* an object to a cell. To do so

1. Choose the <u>T</u>ools⇨<u>O</u>ptions command.

2. Click the Edit tab of the Options dialog box.

3. Place a check mark next to the check box labeled Cut, Copy, and Sort <u>O</u>bjects with Cells.

Graphic objects on the draw layer will be attached to the underlying cells.

Deleting all drawn objects

To delete all objects on a worksheet:

1. Choose the <u>E</u>dit⇨<u>G</u>o To command (or press F5).

2. Click the Special button in the Go To dialog box.

3. Choose the Objects option button and click OK.

All objects will be selected, press Delete to delete them all.

Grouping and ungrouping objects

Excel lets you combine two or more drawn objects into a single object. This is known as *grouping*. You can manipulate a group as a single object (move it, resize it, and so on).

To group two or more objects

1. Select all objects that will be in the group by pressing Ctrl as you click each object.

2. Click the Group tool on the Drawing toolbar.

If you need to modify one of the objects in the group, you can ungroup them:

1. Select the grouped object by clicking it once.

 2. Click the Ungroup tool on the Drawing toolbar.

Excel breaks the object into its original components.

 You also can group and ungroup objects with the Format⇔Placement command or from the shortcut menu that appears when you right-click a selection of objects.

Modifying drawn objects

After you've drawn an object, you can modify it at any time:

1. You can select the object by clicking it once (if the object is not filled with a color or pattern, you must click the object's border).

2. You can make some modifications using the toolbar buttons — for example, changing the fill color.

3. Other modifications require that you use the Format Object dialog box, displayed by any of the following techniques:

   • Select the Format⇔Object command.

   • Press Ctrl+1.

   • Double-click the object.

   • Right-click the object and select Format Object from the shortcut menu.

Moving and resizing drawn objects

To move a drawn object

1. Click the object's border.

2. Drag the object to its desired location.

 If you press Alt while moving an object, the object's upper-left corner will be perfectly aligned to the row and column gridlines.

To change the size or proportions of a drawn object

1. Select the object by clicking it once.

2. Click one of its eight *handles.*

3. Drag until the object is the desired size.

To maintain an object's original proportions when you resize the object, press Shift while dragging any of its borders.

Using clip art

A wide variety of electronic "clip art" is available, and you can use these graphic images in your work without violating any copyright restrictions. Excel can import a wide variety of graphics files, which can be placed on a worksheet's draw layer.

To add a graphic file (clip art) to a worksheet

1. Choose the Insert⇨Picture command.

2. In the Picture dialog box, select the graphic file that you want to use.

3. Click OK to import the image.

After an image is placed on a worksheet, it can be moved.

Remember: Depending on the type of image, resizing may or may not produce good results.

Using bitmap (BMP) graphics in a worksheet can dramatically increase the size of your workbook, resulting in more memory usage and longer load and save times.

See also "Using the Microsoft OLE server applications," in Part VIII and "Applying a background graphic," in Part III.

Using Excel with Other Applications

This part deals with topics related to interacting with other applications. Perhaps the most common application used with a spreadsheet is a word processing program. Data can easily be transferred between these two applications, saving time and maintaining accuracy.

In this part . . .

- ✔ Copying and pasting charts, graphics, text, and data between applications
- ✔ Creating and using links between applications
- ✔ Embedding objects

Copying and Pasting between Applications

Topics in this section deal with *static copying* between applications. In other words, once the information is copied, subsequent changes to the source document will *not* be reflected in the copy of the information.

Remember: Applications vary in how they respond to information copied from the Clipboard. The information here is general; you may need to experiment in order to get the desired effect.

Copying a chart or range of data from Excel to another application

To copy a chart from Excel to another application (such as a word processing document)

1. Make sure the other application is running and the document that you want to copy to is open.

2. Activate Excel.

3. Select the chart or range of data that you want to copy. If the chart is on a separate chart sheet, there's no need to select anything.

4. Choose the Edit⇨Copy command (or press Ctrl+C).

5. Activate the other application (you can use the Windows task bar).

6. Move the cursor to the location where you want to place the copy.

7. Choose the Edit⇨Paste command.

For more control over how the chart and data are pasted, choose the application's Edit⇨Paste Special command (if it has one) in Step 7. The following table describes the effect of choosing the various paste choices in the Word for Windows Paste Special dialog box when the Paste option is selected.

Paste Type	Result
Microsoft Excel Worksheet Object	An object that includes the Excel formatting. This creates an embedded object.
Formatted Text (RTF)	A Word table, formatted as the original Excel range. There is no link to the source. This produces the same result as using the standard Edit⇨Paste command.
Unformatted Text	Text (not a table) that corresponds to Word's Normal style. Formatting from Excel is not transferred, and there is no link to the source.
Picture	A picture object that retains the formatting from Excel. There is no link to the source. This usually produces better results than the Bitmap option. Double-clicking lets you edit the picture.
Bitmap	A bitmap object that retains the formatting from Excel. There is no link to the source. Double-clicking lets you edit the bitmap.

Copying data from another application to Excel

To copy information (either text or numbers) from another application (such as a word processing document) to Excel

1. Make sure Excel is running and the workbook that you want to copy to is open.

2. Activate the other application.

3. Select the information to copy.

4. Choose the Edit⇨Copy command (or press Ctrl+C).

5. Activate Excel (you can use the Windows task bar).

6. Move the cell pointer to the cell where you want to place the copy.

7. Choose the Edit⇨Paste command.

For more control over how the information is pasted, choose Excel's Edit⇨Paste Special command in Step 7.

Remember: The manner in which the data is pasted depends on the application that you are copying from. In some cases you may need to use Excel's Data⇨Text to Columns command to split the information into columns.

See also "Splitting copied data into columns," in this part.

Copying a graphic from another application to Excel

To copy a graphic from another application (such as a drawing program) to Excel

1. Make sure Excel is running and the workbook that you want to copy to is open.

2. Activate the other application.

3. Select the information to copy. This process will vary, depending on the application.

4. Choose the Edit⇨Copy command (or press Ctrl+C).

5. Activate Excel (you can use the Windows task bar).

6. Move the cell pointer to the cell where you want to place the copy.

7. Choose the Edit⇨Paste command.

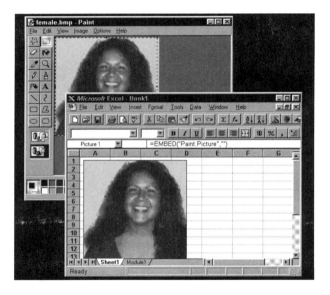

TIP

For more control over how the information is pasted, choose Excel's Edit⇨Paste Special command in Step 7.

Splitting copied data into columns

Sometimes, data copied into an Excel worksheet appears in a single column, when it really should appear in separate columns. To split the data into separate columns

1. Select the data in the single column.

2. Choose the Data⇨Text to Columns command. Excel displays the first of three dialog boxes.

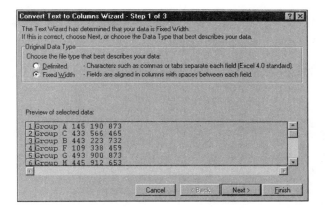

3. Respond to the dialog boxes and click Finish in the last dialog box.

Creating and Using Links between Applications

If you want to share data that may change, you may want to create a *dynamic link* between data copied from one Windows application to another. So, if the data changes in the source document, these changes are made automatically in the destination document.

Remember: Applications vary in how they handle links. The information here is general in nature; you may need to experiment in order to get the desired effect.

Creating a link to another document in Excel

To create a dynamic link in an Excel workbook from a source document

1. Activate the window in the source application that contains the information that you want to copy.

2. Select the information.

3. Select Edit⇨Copy from the source application's menu.

4. Activate Excel (you can use the Windows task bar).

5. Move the cell pointer to the cell where you want to copy.

6. Select the Edit⇨Paste Special command.

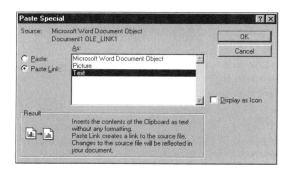

7. In the Paste Special dialog box, select the Paste Link option and choose the appropriate link type in the list box labeled As. These options vary, depending on the source application.

The information is pasted as a single multicell array formula.

Remember: You can format the pasted information, but you cannot edit it in Excel.

See also "Deleting linked information," in this part.

Creating a link to Excel in another document

You may want to create a link to an Excel worksheet in another application, such as a word processing document. To create a dynamic link in another application from an Excel worksheet

1. Select the information in the Excel worksheet.

2. Choose the Edit⇨Copy command.

3. Activate the other application (use the Windows task bar).

4. Move the cursor to the location where you want to copy.

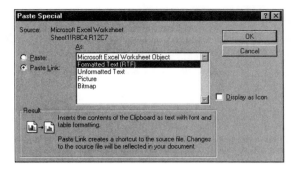

5. Select the application's Edit⇨Paste Special command.

6. In the Paste Special dialog box, select the Paste Link option and choose the appropriate link type in the list box labeled As.

The information is pasted in the document and linked to the worksheet range.

Remember: The exact procedure will vary with the application. The following table describes the effect of choosing the various paste choices in the Word for Windows Paste Special dialog box when the Paste Link option is selected.

Paste Type	Result
Microsoft Excel Worksheet Object	A linked object that includes the Excel formatting. Double-click to edit the source data in Excel.
Formatted Text (RTF)	A Word table formatted as the original Excel range. Changes in the source will be reflected automatically.
Unformatted Text	Text (not a table) that corresponds to Word's Normal style. Formatting from Excel is not transferred. Changes in the source will be reflected automatically.
Picture	A picture object that retains the formatting from Excel. Changes in the source will be reflected automatically. This usually produces better results than the Bitmap option. Double-click to edit the source data in Excel.
Bitmap	A bitmap object that retains the formatting from Excel. Changes in the source will be reflected automatically. Double-click to edit the source data in Excel.

See also: "Embedding an existing workbook in another application," in this part.

Deleting linked information

If you no longer need the information from a linked source document, you can delete the information (and the link). To do so

1. Move the cell pointer to any cell in the linked range.

2. Press Ctrl+/ to select the entire linked range.

3. Press Delete.

See also "Severing (ending) a link," in this part.

Reestablishing a link

If a link becomes severed, you may be able to reestablish it. For example, if you move the source document to another folder, or save it under a different name Excel may not be able to update the link. To reestablish a link

1. Choose the Edit⇨Links command.

2. In the Links dialog box, click the Change Source button.

3. In the Change Links dialog box, edit the reference to refer to the correct file.

4. Click OK to close the Change Links dialog box.

5. Click Close to close the Links dialog box.

The worksheet will be updated with information from the file you specified.

Severing (ending) a link

If you have information in an Excel worksheet that is linked to another document, you may no longer need the link — but want to keep the current information. To sever a link

1. Move the cell pointer to any cell in the linked range.

2. Press Ctrl+/ to select the entire linked range.

3. Choose the Edit⇨Copy command.

4. Choose the Edit⇨Paste Special command.

5. In the Paste Special dialog box, select the Values option.

6. Click OK.

7. Press Esc to exit Copy mode.

The information will appear the same, but it will no longer be linked to the source document.

See also "Deleting linked information," in this part.

Updating a link

Sometimes, a worksheet may not reflect the latest information in a linked document. To update the link

1. Choose the Edit⇨Links command.

2. If there is more than one link, select the appropriate link from the list box in the Links dialog box.

3. Click the Update Now button.

4. Click the Close button to close the Links dialog box.

Embedding Objects

Many applications (including Excel) support embedding — a technique that lets you insert an object from another program and use the other program's editing tools to work with it whenever you want. The embedded objects (sometimes known as OLE objects) can be items such as

✦ Text documents from other products, such as word processors

✦ Drawings or pictures from other products

✦ Information from special *OLE server* applications such as Microsoft Word Art and Microsoft Equation. An OLE server application cannot be used by itself — it must be embedded in another application.

✦ Sound files

✦ Video or animation files

There are three ways to embed an object:

✦ Use the Edit⇨Paste Special command and select the object choice (if it's available). If you do this, select the Paste option rather than the Paste Link option.

✦ Use the Insert⇨Object command.

✦ Drag an object from one application to another.

Remember: Not all applications support all of these methods.

Embedding a new object in a worksheet

To embed a new object (such as an empty word processing document) into a worksheet

1. Move the cell pointer to the location where you want the object.

2. Choose the Insert⇨Object command.

3. In the Object dialog box, click the tab labeled Create New.

4. In the Object Type list box, select the server application.

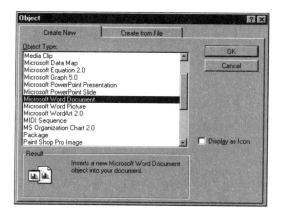

5. Click OK. A new object will be inserted into the workbook. To activate the object, double-click it. You can then work with the object using its native commands.

To return to Excel, click in the worksheet (or, choose the application's File⇨Exit command).

Embedding an empty workbook in another application

To embed a blank Excel workbook into a Word for Windows (or any other application) document:

1. Activate the application. Excel does not need to be running.

2. Move the cursor to the appropriate location.

3. Choose the Insert⇨Object command.

4. In the Object dialog box, click the tab labeled Create New.

5. In the Object Type list box, select Microsoft Excel Worksheet.

6. Click OK. A new workbook will be embedded in the document. To activate the workbook, double-click it. This will give you access to Excel's menus and toolbars.

To return to the word processing document, click anywhere outside of the embedded workbook.

Remember: The exact procedure for embedding a workbook may vary, depending on the application.

See also "Embedding an existing workbook in another application," in this part.

Embedding an existing object in a worksheet

To embed an existing object (such as a word processing document) into a worksheet

1. Move the cell pointer to the location where you want the object.

2. Choose the Insert⇨Object command.

3. In the Object dialog box, click the tab labeled Create from File.

4. In the File Name text box, enter the full path and filename. You can also click the Browse button to locate the file.

5. Click OK. The object will be inserted into the workbook.

To activate the object, double-click it. You can then work with the object using its native commands.

To return to Excel, click in the worksheet (or choose the application's File⇨Exit command).

See also "Embedding a new object in a worksheet," in this part.

Embedding an existing workbook in another application

To embed an existing (or other) Excel workbook into a Word for Windows document

1. Activate the application. Excel does not need to be running.

2. Move the cursor to the appropriate location.

3. Choose the Insert⇨Object command. In the Object dialog box, click the tab labeled Create from File.

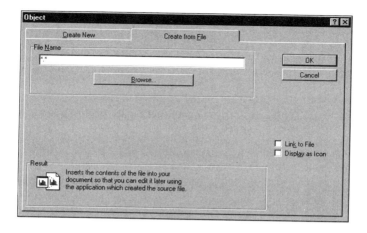

4. In the File Name text box, enter the full path and filename. You can also click the Browse button to locate the file.

5. Click OK. The workbook will be embedded in the document. To activate the workbook, double-click it. This will give you access to Excel's menus and toolbars.

To return to the word processing document, click anywhere outside of the embedded workbook.

Remember: The exact procedure for embedding a workbook may vary, depending on the application.

Using the Microsoft OLE server applications

Microsoft Office includes a few additional applications that you might find useful. These can all be embedded in Excel documents:

◆ **Microsoft Equation:** Lets you create equations.

◆ **Microsoft Word Art:** Lets you modify text in some interesting ways.

◆ **MS Organization Chart:** Lets you create attractive organizational charts.

1. Move the cell pointer to the location where you want the object.

2. Choose the Insert⇨Object command.

3. In the Object dialog box, click the tab labeled Create New.

4. In the Object Type list box, select the server application.

5. Click OK. The object will be inserted into your worksheet. The figure below shows a Word Art object embedded in a worksheet.

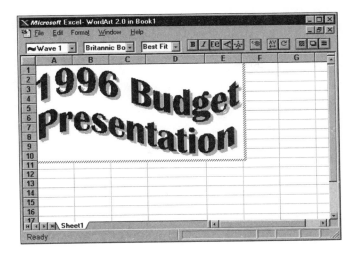

To edit the object, double-click it. You can then use the object's native menus to work with the object.

To return to Excel, click anywhere in the worksheet.

Techie Talk

Absolute reference: In a formula, a reference to a cell that will not change if the formula is copied to a different cell. An absolute reference uses two dollar signs, such as A15 for cell A15.

Active cell: The cell whose contents appears in the formula bar. You can enter information into the active cell and also edit its contents.

Add-in: A file that is loaded into Excel in order to provide additional commands or worksheet functions.

Analysis ToolPak: An add-in that provides Excel with specialized analytical tools and worksheet functions.

Argument: In a worksheet function, information (enclosed in parentheses) that provides details as to what you want the function to do.

Array formula: A special type of formula used by advanced users.

Autofilter: To display only the rows in a list that meet certain criteria.

Autoformat: Predefined formatting that you can quickly apply to a range of cells in a worksheet. Also refers to predefined formats that you can apply to a chart.

Autotemplate: A special type of template that is used as the basis for new workbooks and sheets. Autotemplates are stored in your XLStart folder.

Cell: A single addressable unit in a worksheet, defined by the intersection of a row and column.

Cell note: A note (textual or auditory) that is attached to a cell.

Cell pointer: The dark border that surrounds the active cell. You move the cell pointer with the mouse or the keyboard.

Cell reference: Identifies a cell by giving its column letter and row number. For example, C5 refers to the cell at the intersection of column C and row 5. If you're referring to a cell on a different sheet, you need to precede it with the sheet name and an exclamation point. These can be relative references (most common), absolute references, or mixed references.

Chart: A graphic representation of values in a worksheet. A chart can be embedded on a worksheet or stored on a separate chart sheet in a workbook.

Chart sheet: A type of sheet in a workbook that holds a single chart.

ChartWizard: A series of interactive dialog boxes that help you create charts.

Check box: In a dialog box, an option that can be either on or off. This is not the same as an option button.

Circular reference: In a formula, a reference to the cell that contains the formula (either directly or indirectly). If cell A10 contains **=SUM(A1:A10)**, a circular reference exists because the formula refers to its own cell.

Clipboard: An area of your computer's memory that stores information that has been copied or cut from an application.

Column: Part of a worksheet that consists of 16,384 cells arranged vertically. Each worksheet has 256 columns.

Consolidation: The process of merging data from multiple worksheets or multiple workbook files.

Criteria range: A special type of range that holds specifications used by an advanced filter or for a database worksheet function.

Data table: A table, calculated by Excel, that shows the effects on one or more formulas when one or more input cells take on different values. Excel supports one-way and two-way data tables.

Database: A systematic collection of information comprised of records (rows) and fields (columns). A database can be stored in a worksheet (where it's known as a list) or in an external file.

Dependent cell: A cell that contains a formula that refers to the active cell. In other words, the formula depends on the value in the active cell.

Dialog box: An interactive window that appears in response to most commands. A dialog box is used to get additional information from you so Excel can carry out the command.

Dialog sheet: A sheet in a workbook that contains a custom dialog box. Custom dialog boxes require VBA macros in order to be used.

Double-click: To click the left mouse button rapidly twice.

Drag: To hold down the mouse button to move an object or extend a selection of cells.

Drag-and-drop: To use the mouse to grab something, move it, and drop it somewhere else. You can use drag-and-drop to move a cell, a range, or a graphic object.

Draw layer: An invisible layer on top of all worksheets. The draw layer contains embedded charts, maps, and drawn objects.

Drawn object: A graphic object that you place on the draw layer using one of Excel's drawing tools.

Drop-down list box: In a dialog box, a control that normally only shows one option. If you select this control, it drops down a list to show more options.

Embedded chart: A chart that's placed on a worksheet's draw layer (as opposed to residing on a separate chart sheet).

Export: To save information in a file format that can be used by another application.

Field: In a database, information that is contained in columns.

Fill handle: The small square object that appears at the lower right corner of the active cell or a selected range of cells.

Filter: To hide rows in a list such that only the rows that meet a certain criteria are displayed.

Font: The typeface used for text and values.

Formatting: The process of changing the appearance of a cell, range, or object.

Formula: An entry in a cell that returns a calculated result.

Formula bar: The area of Excel, just below the toolbars, that displays the contents of the active cell. You can edit the cell in the formula bar.

Frozen titles: The process of keeping certain top rows and/or left columns always displayed, no matter where the cell pointer is. You can set this with the Windows⇨Freeze Panes command.

Function: A special keyword that's used in a formula to perform a calculation. Use the Function Wizard to enter a function in a formula.

Function Wizard: A series of interactive dialog boxes that help you enter worksheet functions and their arguments.

Goal seeking: The process of determining the value of a cell that will result in a specific value returned by a formula.

Gridlines: Lines that delineate the cells in a worksheet. In a chart, gridlines are extensions of the tick marks on the axes.

Handles: On graphic objects, these are the small squarish things at the corners and on the sides. You can drag handles with a mouse to change the size of the graphic object.

Icon: A small picture that you can click with your mouse. In this book, a small picture in the left margin that calls your attention to various types of information.

Import: To retrieve information from a file that was saved by another application.

Legend: In a chart, the small box that describes the data series. In a map, the small box that describes the map's contents.

Link formula: A formula that uses a reference to a cell that's contained in a different workbook.

List: A database that's stored in a worksheet. A list contains a header row that describes the contents of the information in each column.

Locked cell: A cell that cannot be changed when the worksheet is protected. If the worksheet is not protected, locked cells can be modified.

Macro: A "program" that automatically executes a series of statements or actions. Macros are used to automate repetitive procedures.

Map: A graphic depiction of data that is based on geography.

Maximize: To make a window as large as it can be.

Menu: A word at the top of Excel's window (just below the title bar). When clicked, a menu displays a series of items.

Menu bar: The series of words at the top of Excel's window (just below the title bar). The menu bar consists of a series of menus.

Menu item: A word displayed when a menu is clicked. Clicking a menu item executes a command in Excel.

Minimize: To make a window as small as it can be.

Mixed reference: In a formula, a reference to a cell that is partially absolute and partially relative. A mixed reference uses one dollar sign, such as A$15 for cell A15. In this case, the column part of the reference is relative; the row part of the reference is absolute.

Mouse pointer: The object that you see move on screen when you move your mouse. The mouse pointer often changes its shape, depending on what you're doing at the time.

Named range: A range that you've assigned a name to. Using named ranges in formulas makes your formulas more readable.

Noncontiguous range: A range of cells that is not contained in a single rectangular area. You select a noncontiguous range by pressing Ctrl while you select cells.

Number format: The manner in which a value is displayed. For example, you can format a number to appear with a percent sign and a specific number of decimal places. The number format changes only the appearance of the number (not the number itself).

OLE object: An object from another application that is stored in a document. OLE stands for Object Linking and Embedding.

Operator: In a formula, a character that represents the type of operation to be performed. Operators include + (plus sign), / (division sign), & (text concatenation), and others.

Option button: In a dialog box, one of a group of buttons. Only one button in the group can be selected at any time.

Outline: A worksheet structured in such a way that information can be expanded (to show additional details) or contracted (to show fewer details).

Page break: A dashed line that appears on-screen to tell you where the pages will break when the worksheet is printed. Page breaks are either natural or can be specified manually.

Pane: One part of a worksheet window that has been split into either two or four parts.

Paste: To retrieve information that was copied or cut and stored on the Clipboard.

Pivot table: A table that summarizes information contained in a worksheet list or external database.

Pointing: The process of selecting a range using either the keyboard or the mouse. When you need to enter a cell or range reference into a dialog box, you can either enter it directly or point to it in the worksheet.

Precedent cell: A cell that is referred to by a formula cell. A single formula can have many precedent cells, and the precedents can be direct or indirect.

Print titles: One or more rows and/or columns that appear on each page of printed output.

Range: A collection of two or more cells. Specify a range by separating the upper left cell and the lower right cell with a colon.

Recalculate: To update a worksheet's formulas using the most current values.

Record: In a database, information that is contained in rows.

Relative reference: In a formula, a reference to a cell that will change (in a relative manner) if the formula is copied to a different cell. A relative reference doesn't use any dollar signs (as opposed to an absolute reference or a mixed reference).

Restore: To return a window (either Excel's window or a workbook window) to its previous size.

Row: Part of a worksheet that consists of 256 cells arranged horizontally. Each worksheet has 16,384 rows.

Scenario: A specific set of values for input cells. Each scenario is assigned a name and can be displayed using Excel's scenario manager.

Scrap: A range of information that is dragged to the Windows desktop. This scrap can then be dragged into another application.

Scroll bar: One of two bars (on the right and bottom of a workbook window) that let you scroll through the worksheet quickly using the mouse.

Selection: The item that is currently activated. A selection can consist of a cell or range, a part of a chart, or one or more graphic objects.

Setup: The name of the program that you run to install Excel. Sometimes you need to re-run Setup to add features that were not installed during the original installation.

Sheet: One unit of a workbook, which can be a worksheet, a chart sheet, a VBA module, a custom dialog sheet, or an Excel 4.0 macro sheet. Activate a sheet by clicking its sheet tab.

Shortcut menu: The context-sensitive menu that appears when you right-click on a cell, range, or object.

Sort: To rearrange the order of rows, based on the contents of one or more columns. Sorts can be in ascending or descending order.

Spreadsheet: A generic term for a product such as Excel that is used to track and calculate data. Or, this term is often used to refer to a worksheet or a workbook.

Status bar: The line at the bottom of the Excel window that shows the status of several things and also displays some messages.

Template: A file that is used as the basis for a new workbook. Examples include the Spreadsheet Solutions templates that come with Excel.

Text attributes: Formats that are applied to cell contents. These include bold, underline, italic, and strikethrough.

Text file: A file that contains data only and no formatting. A text file is sometimes referred to as an ASCII file.

Title bar: The colored bar at the top of every window. You can move a non-maximized window by dragging its title bar with the mouse.

Toolbar: A collection of buttons that serve as shortcuts for common commands.

Undo: To reverse the effects of the last command with the Edit⇨Undo (or Ctrl+Z).

Value: A number entered into a cell.

VBA: Visual Basic for Applications. This is the name of the macro language included with Excel.

VBA module: A sheet in a workbook that contains VBA macros.

What-if analysis: The process of changing one or more input cells and observing the effects on one or more dependent formulas. Excel's Scenario Manager makes it easy to perform what-if analysis.

Window: A container for an application or a workbook. Windows can be moved and resized.

Workbook: The name for a file that Excel uses. A workbook consists of one or more sheets.

Worksheet: A sheet in a workbook that contains cells. Worksheets are the most commonly used sheet type.

Workspace file: A file that contains information about all open workbooks: their size, arrangement, and position. You can save a workspace file and then re-open it to pick up where you left off.

Zoom: To expand or contract the size of the text displayed in a window. Zoom in to make text larger and zoom out to make text smaller so you can see more.

Index

(continued)

(continued)

(continued)